SNAPSHOT

Dublin

CONTENTS

INTRODUCTION

This Snapshot guide, excerpted from the latest edition of my guidebook *Rick Steves' Ireland*, introduces you to the city of Dublin. From its lively pubs filled with Guinness-fueled *craic* (conversation) and traditional music, to its stately Georgian sights, to its powerful rebel history, the Irish capital delights its visitors. Stroll vibrant O'Connell Street for a lesson in Ireland's long struggle for independence, cheer on the local hurling team at Croke Park, and pore over the intricately decorated ninth-century Book of Kells. Pious, earthy, witty, brooding, feisty, and unpretentious, Dublin is an intoxicating potion to sip or slurp—as the mood strikes you.

For a break from the big city, venture to sights near Dublin: the prehistoric tombs at Brú na Bóinne, the site of the pivotal Battle of the Boyne, the stout ruins of Trim Castle, the impressive Gardens of Powerscourt, the monastic settlement at Glendalough, and the proud Irish equestrian tradition at the National Stud.

To help you have the best trip possible, I've included the following topics in this book:

• **Planning Your Time,** with advice on how to make the most of your limited time

• **Orientation,** including tourist information (abbreviated as TI), tips on public transportation, local tour options, and helpful hints

• **Sights** with ratings:

　　　▲▲▲—Don't miss

　　　▲▲—Try hard to see

　　　▲—Worthwhile if you can make it

　　　No rating—Worth knowing about

• **Sleeping** and **Eating,** with good-value recommendations in every price range

• **Connections,** with tips on trains, buses, and driving

• **Practicalities,** near the end of this book, has information on money, phoning, hotel reservations, transportation, and other helpful hints.

To travel smartly, read this little book in its entirety before you go. It's my hope that this guide will make your trip more meaningful and rewarding. Traveling like a temporary local, you'll get the absolute most out of every mile, minute, and euro.

Happy travels!

Rick Steves

DUBLIN

With reminders of its stirring history and rich culture on every corner, Ireland's capital and largest city is a sightseer's delight. Dublin holds its own above its weight class in arts, entertainment, food, and fun. Dublin's fair city will have you humming, "Cockles and mussels, alive, alive-O."

Founded as a Viking trading settlement in the ninth century, Dublin grew to be a center of wealth and commerce, second only to London in the British Empire. Dublin, the seat of English rule in Ireland for 750 years, was the heart of a "civilized" Anglo-Irish area (eastern Ireland) known as "the Pale." Anything "beyond the Pale" was considered uncultured and almost barbaric...purely Irish.

The Golden Age of English Dublin was the 18th century. The British Empire was on a roll, and the city was right there with it. Largely rebuilt during this Georgian era, Dublin—even with its tattered edges—became an elegant and cultured capital.

Those glory days left a lasting imprint on the city. Squares and boulevards built in the Georgian style give the city an air of grandeur (Georgian is British for Neoclassical...named for the period when four consecutive King Georges occupied the British throne). The National Museum, the National Gallery, and many government buildings are in the Georgian section of town. Few buildings (notably Christ Church and St. Patrick's cathedrals) survive from before this Georgian period.

But nationalism—and a realization of the importance of human rights—would forever change Dublin. The American and French revolutions inspired Irish intellectuals to buck British rule, and life in Dublin was never quite the same after the Rebellion of 1798. In 1801, the Act of Union with Britain resulted in the loss of Ireland's parliament (no need for two with the dominant one in London). As the Irish members of parliament moved to Westminster, the movers and shakers of the Anglo-Irish aristocracy followed suit, and Dublin slowly began to decay.

Throughout the 19th century, as Ireland endured the Great Potato Famine and saw the beginnings of the modern struggle for independence, Dublin was treated—and felt—more like a British colony than a partner. The tension culminated in the Easter Uprising of 1916, soon followed by a successful guerilla war of independence against Britain, and Ireland's civil war. With many of its grand streets left in ruins, Dublin emerged as the capital of the British Empire's only former colony in Europe.

While bullet-pocked buildings and dramatic statues keep memories of Ireland's struggle for independence alive, the city is looking ahead to a brighter future. Dubliners are energetic and helpful, while visitors enjoy a big-town cultural scene wrapped in a small-town smile.

Planning Your Time

On a three-week trip through Ireland, Dublin deserves three nights and two days. Be aware that some important sights close on Mondays. Consider this ambitious sightseeing plan:

Day 1:

10:15	Follow the Trinity College guided walk.
11:00	Visit the Book of Kells and Old Library ahead of midday crowds.
12:00	Browse Grafton Street, have lunch there or picnic on St. Stephen's Green.
13:30	See Number Twenty-Nine Georgian House (closed Mon).
15:00	Head to the National Museum: Archaeology branch (also closed Mon).
17:00	Return to hotel, rest, have dinner—eat well for less during early-bird specials.
19:30	Go for an evening guided pub tour (musical or literary).
22:00	Drop in on Irish music in the Temple Bar area.

Day 2:

10:00	Take the Dublin Castle tour.
11:30	Hop on one of the hop-on, hop-off buses, jumping off to see the Guinness Storehouse and Kilmainham Gaol (bring a sandwich to munch in transit on the open-top bus, or stop off to picnic in one of Dublin's green squares).

15:00   Leave the bus at Parnell Square, visit the Garden of Remembrance, and stroll down to O'Connell Bridge, sightseeing and shopping as you like along the way.

Evening   Catch a play, concert, or Comhaltas traditional music in Dun Laoghaire.

With More Time: Dublin, while relatively small, can keep you busily sightseeing for days without even leaving the center of town. And with all its music, theater, and after-hours tours—not to mention the lively pub scene—evenings are just as fun.

Orientation to Dublin

(area code: 01)
Greater Dublin sprawls with 1.2 million people—more than a quarter of the country's population. But the center of tourist interest is a

tight triangle between O'Connell Bridge, St. Stephen's Green, and Christ Church Cathedral. Within this triangle you'll find Trinity College (Book of Kells), Grafton Street (top pedestrian shopping zone), Temple Bar (trendy and touristy nightlife center), Dublin Castle, and the hub of most city tours and buses. The only major sights outside this easy-to-walk triangle are the Kilmainham Gaol, the Guinness Storehouse, and the National Museum: Decorative Arts and History branch (all west of the center).

The River Liffey cuts the town in two. Focus on the southern half, where most of your sightseeing will take place. Dublin's wide main drag, O'Connell Street, starts north of the river at the Parnell monument and runs south, down to the central O'Connell Bridge. After crossing the bridge, it continues south as the major city axis past Trinity College and through pedestrian-only Grafton Street to St. Stephen's Green. Get used to the fact that many long Dublin streets change their names every few blocks. A prime example of this are the numerously named Quays (pronounced "keys"), which run east-west along the River Liffey.

The suburban port of Dun Laoghaire (dun LEERY) lies south of Dublin, 25 minutes away by DART commuter train. Travelers connecting by ferry to Holyhead in Wales—or those just looking for a mellow town to sleep in outside of urban Dublin—can easily home-base here. Another option is the northern suburb of Howth, also 25 minutes away on the DART and closer to the airport. Room prices are about one-fourth cheaper in Dun Laoghaire or Howth than in downtown Dublin.

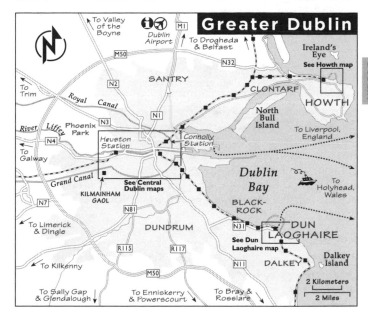

DUBLIN

Tourist Information

Dublin's main tourist information office (TI) is a thriving hub of ticket and info desks filling an old church (Mon-Sat June-Sept 9:00-17:30, Oct-May 9:30-17:30; Sun 10:30-15:00 year-round; a block off Grafton Street on Suffolk Street, tel. 01/850-230-330 or 01/605-7700, www.visitdublin.com). It has a bus-info desk, sandwich bar, more maps and books than you'll ever need, and racks advertising the busy entertainment scene. You can buy tickets to many theater and concert events here. It's also a good place to pick up brochures for destinations throughout Ireland. There's another TI at the airport (daily 8:00-20:00, Terminal 1) and one at the Dun Laoghaire ferry terminal (Mon-Sat 9:30-12:45 & 14:00-17:30, closed Sun). A smaller satellite TI is halfway down the east side of O'Connell Street (Mon-Sat 9:00-17:00, closed Sun).

Pick up the TI's *The Guide,* which includes a decent city map (free). Inside is a minimal schedule of happenings in town. The excellent *Collins Illustrated Discovering Dublin Map* (€7 at TIs and newsstands) is the ultimate city map, listing just about everything of interest, along with helpful opinions and tidbits of Dublin history.

Dublin Pass: This sightseeing pass is a good deal only if you like to visit lots of sights quickly (€35/1 day, €55/2 days, €65/3 days, €95/6 days, sold at TIs, www.dublinpass.ie). The pass saves a few minutes, when you'd otherwise need to wait in line to buy a ticket. It covers 32 museums, churches, litera-

DUBLIN

ture-related sights, and expensive stops such as the Guinness Storehouse and the Old Jameson Distillery, plus the Aircoach airport bus—one-way from the airport to the city only (doesn't cover Airlink buses). However, the pass doesn't include the famous Book of Kells at Trinity College or any bus tours or walking tours. Note that some of the sights it claims to "cover"— such as the National Gallery, the Chester Beatty Library, and the National Museum's Archaeology and Decorative Arts and History branches—are actually free (although passholders get other benefits that regular visitors won't, such as a free glossy guide at the National Gallery that normally costs €5). The booklet that comes with the pass can be a handy planning tool. But the bottom line is that most travelers won't get their money's worth out of this pass.

Arrival in Dublin

By Train

Dublin has two train stations. **Heuston Station,** on the west end of town, serves west and southwest Ireland (30-minute walk from O'Connell Bridge; take taxi or bus #90—see below). **Connolly Station,** which serves the north, northwest, and Rosslare, is closer to the center (10-minute walk from O'Connell Bridge). Each station has ATMs, but only Heuston has lockers (small lockers-€4/day, large-€6/day, 7-day maximum).

The two train stations are connected by the red line of the LUAS commuter train (see "Getting Around Dublin") and by bus. Bus #90 runs along the river, linking both train stations, the bus station, and the city center (€1.20, 6/hour).

To reach Heuston Station from the city center, catch bus #90 on the south side of the river; to get to Connolly Station and Busáras Central Bus Station from the city center, catch #90 on the north side of the river.

By Bus

Bus Éireann, Ireland's national bus company, uses the **Busáras** (Bu-SAUR-us...like a dinosaur) **Central Bus Station** next to Connolly Station. It's a 10-minute walk, or a short ride on bus #90 (described above), to the city center.

By Plane

The airport has two terminals: the new Terminal 2, which serves American carriers (Delta, United, Continental, American, and US Airways), plus most Aer Lingus flights. Terminal 1 serves Ryanair, Aer Arann, Air Canada, Aer Lingus (some regional flights), and most European carriers, including British Midland, SAS, Lufthansa, Air France, Swiss Air, and Iberia. Airport tel. 01/814-

1111, www.dublinairport.ie.

Both terminals, which are located an easily walkable 150 yards apart, have ATMs, exchange bureaus, cafés, Wi-Fi, and luggage storage. At Terminal 1, the left-luggage office (daily 6:00-23:00) is across the street in the Short-Term Car Park Atrium, along with a small supermarket. Terminal 1 also has a TI (daily 8:00-20:00), pharmacy, bus-and-rail info desk, and car-rental agencies (on ground/arrivals level).

Getting Downtown by Bus: You have two main choices: Airlink (double-decker green bus) or Aircoach (single-deck blue bus). Both pick up on the street directly in front of airport arrivals, at ground level at both terminals. Consider buying a €13.30 **Rambler** city-bus pass at the airport TI, which covers the Airlink bus into town—but read the following description first to make sure Airlink is the best choice for your trip.

Airlink: Airlink bus #747 stops at both airport terminals, linking the airport to the city center along a strip a few blocks north and south of the river. The route includes the Busáras Central Bus Station, Connolly Station, O'Connell Street, Trinity College, Christchurch, and Heuston Station. Ask the driver which stop is closest to your hotel (€6, pay driver, 3/hour, 35-45 minutes, tel. 01/873-4222, www.dublinbus.ie).

Aircoach: To reach recommended hotels near St. Stephen's Green (south of the city center), the Aircoach bus is best (€7, covered by Dublin Pass, 3/hour, runs 5:00-23:30; pay driver and confirm best stop for your hotel, tel. 01/844-7118, www.aircoach.ie).

City Bus: The cheapest (and slowest) way from the airport to downtown Dublin is by city bus; buses marked #16A, #41, #41A, and #41B go to O'Connell Street (€2.30, exact change required, no change given, 4/hour, 55 minutes, tel. 01/873-4222, www.dublin bus.ie).

Getting to Dun Laoghaire by Bus: The best way to get to Dun Laoghaire is to take the **Aircoach bus** (€8, hourly, 50 minutes, tel. 01/844-7118, www.aircoach.ie).

Taking a Taxi: Taxis from the airport into Dublin cost about €35; to Dun Laoghaire, about €50; to Howth, about €25.

By Ferry

Irish Ferries dock at the mouth of the River Liffey (at Dublin Docklands, near the town center), while the **Stena Line** docks at Dun Laoghaire (easy DART train connections into Dublin, 4/hour, 25 minutes).

By Car

Trust me: You don't want to drive in downtown Dublin. Cars are unnecessary for sightseeing in town, parking is expensive (about

€25/day), and traffic will get your fighting Irish up. Save your car-rental days for cross-country travel between smaller towns and see this energetic city by taxi, bus, or on foot. If you have a car, sleep out in the suburbs (Dun Laoghaire or Howth), and ask your inn-keeper about the best places to park.

Drivers renting a car at Dublin Airport, but not staying in Dun Laoghaire or Howth, can bypass the worst of the big-city traffic by taking the M50 ring road south or west. The M50 uses an automatic tolling system called eFlow. Your rented car should already come with an eFlow tag installed; however, confirm this when you pick up your car at the airport. The €2.50 toll per trip is automatically debited from the credit card that you used to rent the car (for pass details, see www.eflow.ie).

Helpful Hints

High Costs: Despite the busted Celtic Tiger economic boom (1995-2007—R.I.P.), Ireland is still one of the EU's more expensive countries. Restaurants and lodging—other than hostels—are more expensive the closer you get to the tour-isty Temple Bar district. A pint of beer in a Temple Bar pub costs almost €6 (a sobering thought).

Pickpockets: Irish destinations, especially Dublin, are not immune to this scourge. Wear a money belt or risk spend-ing a couple of days of your cherished vacation in bureau-cratic purgatory—on the phone canceling credit cards and at the embassy waiting for a replacement passport (see below). Wasting vacation time this way is like paying to wait in line at the DMV.

Tourist Victim Support Service: This service can be helpful if you run into any problems (Mon-Sat 10:00-18:00, Sun 12:00-18:00, tel. 01/478-5295, www.itas.ie).

US Embassy: It's on 42 Elgin Road in the Ballsbridge neighbor-hood (Mon-Tue and Thu-Fri 8:30-11:30 for passport concerns, closed Wed and Sat-Sun, tel. 01/668-7122 or 01/668-8777, http://dublin.usembassy.gov).

Festivals: Book ahead during festivals and for any weekend. St. Patrick's Day is a four-day extravaganza in Dublin (March 16-19 in 2012, www.stpatricksday.ie). June 16 is Bloomsday, dedicated to the Irish author James Joyce and featuring the Messenger Bike Rally (www.jamesjoyce.ie). Hotels raise their prices and are packed on rugby weekends (about four per year), during the all-Ireland Gaelic football and hurl-ing finals (Sundays in September), and during summer rock concerts.

Meet a Dubliner: The **City of a Thousand Welcomes** offers a

DUBLIN

free service that brings together volunteers and first-time visitors for a cup of tea or a pint. Visitors sign up online in advance, pick an available time slot, and meet their Dublin "ambassador" at the Little Museum of Dublin on St. Stephen's Green. You'll head for a nearby tearoom or pub and enjoy a short, informal conversation to get you oriented to the city (free, must be at least 21, 15 St. Stephens Green, tel. 01/661-1000, mobile 087-131-7129, www.cityofathousand welcomes.com).

Internet Access: Internet cafés have sprung up on nearly every street. **Viva Internet** is close to Christ Church Cathedral (Mon-Thu 10:00-22:00, Fri-Sat 10:30-22:00, Sun 12:00-22:00, Lord Edward Street near City Hall, tel. 01/672-4725). **Central Internet Café** is aptly named (Mon-Fri 9:00-22:00, Sat 11:00-19:00, Sun 12:00-18:00, 6 Grafton Street, easy-to-miss door is directly opposite AIB Bank, tel. 01/677-8298, www.centralinternetcafe.com). **Global Internet Café** is north of the River Liffey (Mon-Fri 8:00-23:00, Sat 9:00-23:00, Sun 10:00-23:00, 8 Lower O'Connell Street, tel. 01/878-0295).

Laundry: Patrick Street Launderette, a block southwest of Jurys Inn Christ Church on Patrick Street, is full-service only. Allow four hours and about €10 for a load (Mon-Fri 9:00-20:00, Sat 9:00-18:00, closed Sun, tel. 01/473-1779). The **All-American Launderette** offers self- and full-service options (Mon-Sat 8:30-19:00, Sun 10:00-18:00, 40 South Great George's Street, tel. 01/677-2779).

Bike Rental (Not): Dublin has joined other enlightened European cities in encouraging bike-riding to relieve urban traffic. There are 40-some stations of durable new dublinbikes (dbs) scattered across the city—locals can pick up a bike at any station and turn it in at another. Unfortunately for us, the kiosks only take chip-and-PIN credit cards, not regular US cards. Despite the variable weather and potential for vandalism, this city program has proven to be an early success in reducing congestion.

Getting Around Dublin

You'll do most of Dublin on foot, though when you need public transportation, you'll find it readily available and easy to use.

By Bus: Buses are cheap and cover the city thoroughly. Most lines start at the four quays, or piers, that are nearest to O'Connell Bridge. If you're away from the center, nearly any bus takes you back downtown. Some bus stops are "request only" stops: Be alert to the bus numbers (above the windshield) of approaching buses. When you see your bus coming, extend your arm straight out with your palm toward the bus (the usual hand sign that signals "stop") to flag it down. Tell the driver where you're going, and he'll ask for €1.20-2.30 depending on the number of stops. Bring change or lose any excess. Bus #90 connects the bus and train stations.

The bus office at 59 Upper O'Connell Street has free bus-route maps and sells two different city-bus passes (Mon 8:30-17:30, Tue-Fri 9:00-17:30, Sat 9:00-14:00, Sun 9:30-14:00, tel. 01/873-4222, www.dublinbus.ie). The three-day **Rambler pass** costs €13.30 and covers the Airlink airport bus (but not Aircoach buses or DART trains). The one-day **Short Hop pass,** which costs €10.70, includes DART trains (but not Airlink or Aircoach buses). Passes are also sold at each TI, and at newsstands and markets citywide (mostly Centra, Mace, Spar, and Londis).

By DART (Train): Speedy commuter trains run along the coast, connecting Dublin with Dun Laoghaire's ferry terminal, Howth's harbor, and recommended B&Bs. Think of the DART line as a giant "C" that serves coastal suburbs from Bray in the south to Howth in the north (€2.40, €4.20 round-trips valid same day only, Eurailpass valid but you'll use up a valuable flexi-day, tel. 01/703-3504, www.irishrail.ie/home).

By LUAS (Light Rail): The city's light-rail system has two main lines (red and green) that serve inland suburbs. The more useful line for tourists is the red line, connecting the Heuston and Connolly train stations (a 15-minute ride apart) at either edge of the Central 1 Zone. In between, the Busáras Central Bus Station, Smithfield, and Museum stops can be handy (€1.50, 6/hour, runs 5:30-24:30, tel. 1-800-300-604, www.luas.ie). Check the 15-foot-high pillars at each boarding platform that display the time and destination of the next LUAS train. Make sure you're on the right platform for the direction you want to go.

By Taxi: Taxis are everywhere and easy to hail (cheaper for 3-4 people). Cabbies are generally honest, friendly, and good sources of information (€4.10 daytime minimum 8:00-20:00, €4.45 nighttime minimum 20:00-8:00, €1 for each additional adult, figure about €10 for most crosstown rides, €40/hour for guided joyride). If you call to arrange a pickup (for example, from your hotel), they'll tack on a €2 fee.

Tours in Dublin

While Dublin's physical treasures are lackluster by European standards, the city has a fine story to tell and people with a natural knack for telling it. It's a good town for walking tours, and the competition is fierce. Dublin is noisy; if you can't hear the guide, move in closer. Pamphlets touting creative walks are posted all over town. Choices include medieval walks, literary walks, Georgian Dublin walks, traditional music pub crawls, and even a rock-and-stroll walk tracing the careers of contemporary Irish bands. Taking an evening walk is a great way to meet other travelers. The Dublin TI also offers series of free, good-quality "iWalks" for travelers with iPods or other MP3 players (download with maps at www .visitdublin.com).

By Foot

▲▲Historical Walking Tour—This is your best introductory walk. A group of hardworking history graduates—many of whom claim to have done more than just kiss the Blarney Stone—enliven Dublin's basic historic strip (Trinity College, Old Parliament House, Dublin Castle, and Christ Church Cathedral). You'll get the story of their city, from its Viking origins to the present. Guides speak at length about the roots of Ireland's struggle with Britain. As you listen to your guide, you'll stand in front of buildings that aren't much to look at, but are lots to talk about (May-Sept daily at 11:00 and 15:00, April and Oct daily at 11:00, Nov-March Fri-Sun only at 11:00). All walks last two hours and cost €12 (but get the €10 "student" discount rate with this book in 2012, free for kids under 14, departs from front gate of Trinity College, private tours available, mobile 087-688-9412 or 087-830-3523, www.historical insights.ie).

▲▲▲Traditional Irish Musical Pub Crawl—This impressive and entertaining tour visits the upstairs rooms of three pubs; there, you'll listen to two musicians talk about, play, and sing traditional Irish music. While having only two musicians makes the music a bit thin (Irish music aficionados will say you're better

ter off just finding a good session), the evening—though touristy—is not gimmicky. It's an education in traditional Irish music. The musicians, who also demonstrate a few instruments, clearly enjoy introducing rookies to their art and are very good at it. In the summer, this popular tour frequently sells out —reserve ahead (€12, €1 discount with this book in 2012, beer extra, allow 2.5 hours, April-Oct daily at 19:30, Nov-March Thu-Sat only, maximum 50 tourists, meet upstairs at Gogarty's Pub at the corner of Fleet and Anglesea in the Temple Bar area, tel. 01/475-3313, www.musical pubcrawl.com).

DUBLIN

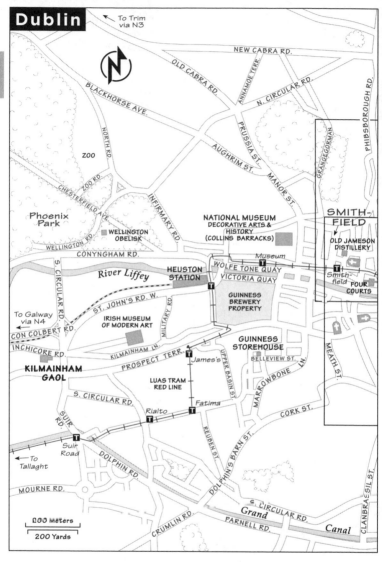

▲Dublin Literary Pub Crawl—Two actors take 40 or so tourists on a walk, stopping at four pubs. Their clever banter introduces the novice to the high *craic* of James Joyce, Seán O'Casey, and W. B. Yeats. The two-hour tour is punctuated with 20-minute pub breaks (free time). While the beer lubricates the social fun, it dilutes the content of the evening. (If you want straight lit and drama, find a real performance; there are many throughout the summer, such as the lunchtime hour on weekends at 13:00 at the Dublin Writers'

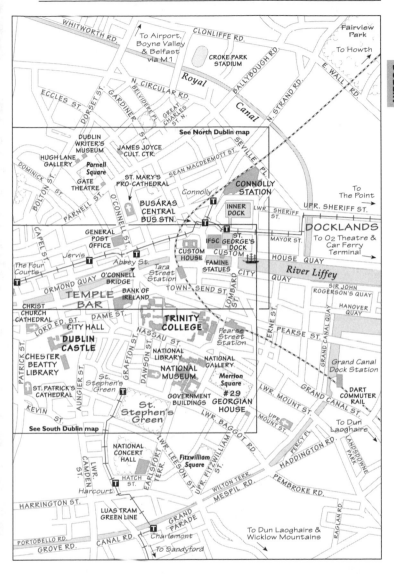

Museum.) However, the pub crawl is an easygoing excuse to drink beer in busy pubs, hook up with other travelers, and get a dose of Irish witty lit (€13, €1 discount with this book in hand in 2012, April-Oct daily at 19:30, Nov-March Thu-Sun at 19:30; you can normally just show up, but call ahead July-Aug when it can fill up; meet upstairs in the Duke Pub—off Grafton on Duke Street, tel. 01/670-5602, mobile 087-263-0270, www.dublinpubcrawl .com). Connoisseurs of Irish pubs will want to buy the excellent

Dublin Literary Pub Crawl guidebook by pub-crawl founder Colm Quilligan.

1916 Rebellion Walking Tour—This two-hour walk breathes gritty life into the most turbulent year in modern Irish history, when idealistic Irish rebels launched the Easter Uprising— eventually leading to independence from Britain. Guide Lorcan Collins has written a guidebook called *The Easter Rising*—worth seeking out—and is passionate about his walks (€12, €2 discount with this book in 2012, daily March-Oct Mon-Sat at 11:30, Sun at 13:00, no tours Nov-mid-March, depart from International Bar at 23 Wicklow Street, mobile 086-858-3847, www.1916rising.com).

Pat Liddy's Walking Tours—Trained by one of Dublin's top historians, these guides take small groups on enthusiastic and informal two-hour walks of various neighborhoods. Each tour has a different focus, such as Viking & Medieval, Georgian Dublin, or Castle & Cathedral (€6-12, depends on tour and admission fees— see website; mid-April-Oct daily at 10:00, 11:00, 14:00, and 15:00; meet in front of TI on Suffolk Street, tel. 01/832-9406 or mobile 087-905-2480, www.walkingtours.ie).

Rebel Tours of Dublin—These 1.5-hour walks focus on revolutionary events in Dublin from 1913 to 1923 as Ireland shed British rule. Strongly opinionated, these guides view history through the lens of Irish Republicanism (€10, departs Mon-Sat at 11:30 from Sinn Fein Bookshop at 58 Parnell Square, tel. 01/814-8542).

By Bike

Dublin City Bike Tours—You'll "get your craic on a saddle" with Dublin City Bike Tours as you pedal across this flat city on innovative urban bikes. Their fun tours visit 20 points of interest north and south of the River Liffey, covering more ground (five miles) than walking tours. Designed for riders of average fitness, they set a casual pace, and rarely let a little rain stop them (€24; includes bike, helmet, insurance, snacks, and water; €4 discount with this book—show when you pay, cash only, reserve in advance, 2.5 hours, March-Nov daily at 10:00 and 14:00, May-Oct also at 18:00, depart Isaac's Hostel a half-block west of Busáras Central Bus Station at 2-5 Frenchman's Lane, mobile 087-134-1866, www.dublincitybiketours.com).

By Bus (on Land and Water)

▲**Hop-on, Hop-off Bus Tours**—Two companies (Dublin Bus Tour and City Sightseeing Dublin) offer hop-on, hop-off bus tours of Dublin, doing virtually identical 1.5-hour circuits. You can get on or off at your choice of about 20 stops (€16, 4/hour, daily 9:30-17:00, buy ticket on board, valid for 48 hours). Buses are mostly

topless, with live running commentaries. This type of tour, which runs in many European cities but isn't always well executed, is made-to-order for Dublin, and buses run so frequently that they make your sightseeing super-efficient. Stops include the far-flung Guinness Storehouse and Kilmainham Gaol, although the Dublin Bus Tour stops a few blocks from the Gaol.

Dublin Bus Tour (green buses) drivers provide fun and quirky narration (tel. 01/873-4222, www.dublinsightseeing.ie). **City Sightseeing Dublin** (red buses) come with both a guide and a driver, rather than just a driver who guides (tel. 01/872-9010, www.irishcitytours.com).

Each company's map, free with your ticket, details various discounts that you'll get at Dublin's sights (such as the Guinness Storehouse, Viking Splash tour, Old Jameson Distillery, Dublin Writers' Museum, Dublinia, Christ Church Cathedral, and others). To take advantage of the discounts, take a bus tour before you do all of your sightseeing.

▲**Viking Splash Tours**—If you'd like to ride in a WWII amphibious vehicle—driven by a Viking-costumed guide who's as liable to spout history as he is to growl—this is for you. The tour starts with a group roar from the Viking within us all. At first, the guide talks as if he were a Viking ("When we came here in 841..."), but soon the patriot emerges as he tags Irish history onto the sights you pass. Near the end of the 1.25-hour tour (punctuated by occasional group roars at passersby), you don a life jacket for a slow spin up and down a boring canal. Although it's covered, the boat is breezy—dress appropriately. Kids who expect a Viking splash may feel like they've been trapped in a classroom, but historians will enjoy the talk more than the gimmick (€20, Feb-Nov daily 10:00-17:00, none Dec-Jan, departs about hourly from the north side of St. Stephen's Green opposite Dawson Street, ticket office at 64-65 Patrick Street, tel. 01/707-6000, www.vikingsplash.com).

Weekend Tour Packages for Students in Dublin

Andy Steves (Rick's son) runs Weekend Student Adventures, offering experiential three-day weekend tours for €250, designed for American students studying abroad (www.wsaeurope.com for details on tours of Dublin and other great cities).

Dublin at a Glance

▲▲▲**Traditional Irish Musical Pub Crawl** A fascinating, practical, and enjoyable primer on traditional Irish music. **Hours:** April-Oct daily at 19:30, Nov-March Thu-Sat only. See page 11.

▲▲▲**National Museum: Archaeology** Interesting collection of Irish treasures from the Stone Age to today. **Hours:** Tue-Sat 10:00-17:00, Sun 14:00-17:00, closed Mon. See page 19.

▲▲▲**Kilmainham Gaol** Historic jail used by the British as a political prison—today a museum that tells a moving story of the suffering of the Irish people. **Hours:** Daily 9:30-18:00. See page 38.

▲▲**Historical Walking Tour** Your best introduction to Dublin. **Hours:** May-Sept daily at 11:00 and 15:00, April and Oct daily at 11:00, Nov-March Fri-Sun only at 11:00. See page 11.

▲▲**Trinity College Tour** Ireland's most famous school, best visited with a 30-minute tour led by one of its students. **Hours:** May-Sept daily 10:15-15:40, Feb-April and Oct-Nov Sat-Sun only, no tours Dec-Jan; weather permitting. See page 18.

▲▲**Book of Kells in the Trinity Old Library** An exquisite illuminated manuscript, the most important piece of art from the Dark Ages. **Hours:** May-Sept daily 9:30-16:30; Oct-April Mon-Sat 9:30-16:30, Sun 12:00-16:30. See page 18.

▲▲**Number Twenty-Nine Georgian House** Restored 18th-century house; tours provide an intimate glimpse of middle-class Georgian life. **Hours:** Tue-Sat 10:00-17:00, Sun 12:00-17:00, closed Mon. See page 22.

▲▲**Grafton Street** The city's liveliest pedestrian shopping mall. **Hours:** Always open. See page 23.

▲▲**Dublin Castle** The city's historic 700-year-old castle, featuring ornate English state apartments, tourable only with a guide. **Hours:** Mon-Sat 10:00-16:45, Sun 12:00-16:45. See page 24.

▲▲**Chester Beatty Library** American expatriate's eclectic yet sumptuous collection of literary and religious treasures from Islam, the Orient, and medieval Europe. **Hours:** May-Sept Mon-Fri 10:00-17:00, Sat 11:00-17:00, Sun 13:00-17:00; Oct-April Tue-Fri 10:00-17:00, Sat 11:00-17:00, Sun 13:00-17:00, closed Mon. See page 24.

▲▲**Temple Bar** Dublin's trendiest neighborhood, with shops, cafés, theaters, galleries, pubs, and restaurants—a great spot for live traditional music. **Hours:** Always open. See page 27.

▲▲**O'Connell Bridge** Landmark bridge spanning the River Liffey at the center of Dublin. **Hours:** Always open. See page 28.

▲▲**O'Connell Street** Dublin's grandest promenade and main drag, packed with history and ideal for a stroll. **Hours:** Always open. See page 29.

▲**National Gallery** Fine collection of top Irish painters and European masters. **Hours:** Mon-Sat 9:30-17:30, Thu until 20:30, Sun 12:00-17:30. See page 21.

▲**Merrion Square** Enjoyable and inviting park with a fun statue of Oscar Wilde. **Hours:** Always open. See page 22.

▲**St. Stephen's Green** Relaxing park surrounded by fine Georgian buildings. **Hours:** Always open. See page 23.

▲**Dublinia** A fun, kid-friendly look at Dublin's Viking and medieval past with a side order of archaeology and a cool town model. **Hours:** Daily March-Sept 10:00-17:00, Oct-Feb 11:00-16:30. See page 26.

▲**Guinness Storehouse** The home of Ireland's national beer, with a museum of beer-making, a gallery of clever ads, and the spectacular Gravity Bar with panoramic city views. **Hours:** Daily 9:30-17:00, July-Aug until 19:00. See page 39.

▲**National Museum: Decorative Arts and History** Shows off Irish dress, furniture, silver, and weaponry with a special focus on the 1916 rebellion, fight for independence, and civil war. **Hours:** Tue-Sat 10:00-17:00, Sun 14:00-17:00, closed Mon. See page 40.

▲**Gaelic Athletic Association Museum** High-tech museum of traditional Gaelic sports such as hurling and Irish football. **Hours:** July-Aug Mon-Sun 9:30-18:00; Sept-June Mon-Sat 9:30-17:00, Sun 12:00-17:00. On game Sundays, it's open only to ticket-holders. See page 41.

DUBLIN

Sights in Dublin

South of the River Liffey
Trinity College

Founded in 1592 by Queen Elizabeth I to establish a Protestant way of thinking about God, Trinity has long been Ireland's most prestigious college. Originally, the student body was limited to rich Protestant males. Women were admitted in 1903, and Catholics—though allowed entrance by the school much earlier—were only given formal permission by the Catholic Church to study at Trinity in the 1970s. Today, half of Trinity's 12,500 students are women, and 70 percent are culturally Catholic (although only about 20 percent of Irish youth are churchgoing).

▲▲**Trinity College Tour**—Trinity students organize and lead 30-minute **tours** of their campus

(look just inside the gate for posted departure times and a ticket-seller on a stool). You'll get a rundown of the mostly Georgian architecture; a peek at student life past and present; and the enjoyable company of your guide, a witty Irish college kid.

Cost and Hours: €10, includes €9 fee to see Book of Kells, where the tour leaves you; May-Sept daily 10:15-15:40, Feb-April and Oct-Nov Sat-Sun only, no tours Dec-Jan, departs roughly every 30 minutes, weather permitting.

▲▲**Book of Kells in the Trinity Old Library**—The only Trinity campus interior welcoming tourists is the Old Library (just follow the signs), with its precious Book of Kells. Written on vellum (calfskin) in the late eighth century—by Irish monks on the island of Iona, Scotland—this enthusiastically decorated copy of the four Gospels was taken safely inland to the Irish monastery at Kells in A.D. 806 after a series of Viking raids. Arguably the finest piece of art from what is generally called the Dark Ages, the Book of Kells shows that monastic life in this far fringe of Europe was far from dark.

The first-class "Turning Darkness into Light" **exhibit,** with a one-way route, puts the 680-page illuminated manuscript in its historical and cultural context, preparing you to see the original book and other precious manuscripts in the treasury. Make a point to spend time in the exhibit (before reaching the actual Book of Kells). Especially interesting are the five-minute video clips showing the exacting care that went into transcribing the monk-uscripts and the ancient art of bookbinding. Two small TV screens (on opposite walls of the exhibition room) run continuously, silently demonstrating the monks' labors of love.

The manuscript has been bound into four separate volumes, and at any given time, two of the four gospels are on display in the **treasury.** The crowd around the one glass case that displays the treasures can be off-putting, but hold your own and get up close. You'll see four richly decorated, 1,200-year-old pages—two text and two decorated cover pages. The library treasury also displays two other books—likely the Book of Armagh (A.D. 807) and the Book of Durrow (A.D. 680)—neither of which can be checked out.

Next, a stairway leads upstairs to the 200-foot-long main chamber of the Old Library (from 1732), stacked to its towering ceiling with 200,000 of the library's oldest books. Here, you'll find one of a dozen surviving original copies of the **Proclamation of the Irish Republic.** Patrick Pearse read these words outside the General Post Office on April 24, 1916, starting the Easter Uprising that led to Irish independence. Read the entire thing...imagining it was yours. Notice the inclusive opening phrase and the seven signatories (each of whom was executed).

Another national icon is nearby: the 15th-century **Brian Boru harp,** the oldest surviving Irish harp (its name is misleading—the Irish High King Brian Boru died 400 years before the harp was created). The Irish love of music is so intense that Ireland is the only nation with a musical instrument as its national symbol. You'll see this harp's likeness everywhere, including on the back of all Irish euro coins and government documents. The harp's inspirational effect on Gaelic culture was so strong that Queen Elizabeth I, who tried to eradicate the Gaelic culture during her reign (1558-1603), ordered Irish harpists to be hung wherever found and their instruments smashed.

Cost and Hours: €9, included in €10 Trinity College tour—see earlier, audioguide-€5; May-Sept daily 9:30-16:30; Oct-April Mon-Sat 9:30-16:30, Sun 12:00-16:30; tel. 01/896-2320, www.tcd.ie/library/bookofkells. A long line often snakes out of the building. Minimize your wait by avoiding the midday crunch (roughly 11:00-14:30).

Museums South of Trinity College
▲▲▲**National Museum: Archaeology**—Showing off the treasures of Ireland from the Stone Age to modern times, this

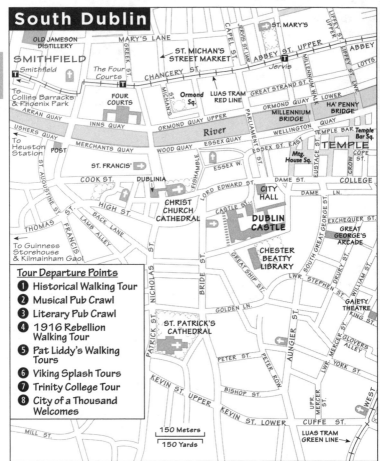

South Dublin

OLD JAMESON DISTILLERY

SMITHFIELD

Smithfield

To Collins Barracks & Phoenix Park

MARY'S LANE

GREEK ST.

The Four Courts

CHANCERY ST.

FOUR COURTS

ARRAN QUAY

INNS QUAY

USHERS QUAY

To Heuston Station

MERCHANTS QUAY

ST. AUGUSTINE ST.

POST

ST. FRANCIS'

COOK ST.

DUBLINIA

THOMAS

HIGH ST.

BACK LANE

LAMB ALLEY

FRANCIS ST.

To Guinness Storehouse & Kilmainham Gaol

ST. MICHAN'S STREET MARKET

ST. MARY'S

CAPEL ST.

JERVIS ST.

ABBEY ST. UPPER

ABBEY

LOTTS

Jervis

Ormond Sq.

MICHAN'S

LUAS TRAM RED LINE

GREAT STRAND ST.

PARLIAMENT ST.

ORMOND QUAY UPPER

ORMOND QUAY LOWER

MILLENNIUM WALK

River

WOOD QUAY

ESSEX QUAY

FISHAMBLE

WELLINGTON

MILLENNIUM BRIDGE

HA' PENNY BRIDGE

QUAY

TEMPLE BAR

Temple Bar Sq.

TEMPLE

ESSEX ST. EAST

ESSEX W.

Mtg. House Sq.

EUSTACE ST.

COPE ST.

CROW ST.

DAME ST.

COLLEGE

LORD EDWARD ST.

CITY HALL

DAME LN.

CHRIST CHURCH CATHEDRAL

HIGH ST.

CASTLE ST.

DUBLIN CASTLE

DAME

SOUTH GREAT GEORGE'S ST.

EXCHEQUER ST.

GREAT GEORGE'S ARCADE

NICHOLAS ST.

BRIDE ST.

CHESTER BEATTY LIBRARY

GREAT SHIP ST.

LWR. STEPHEN ST.

DRURY ST.

WILLIAM ST.

Tour Departure Points

1 Historical Walking Tour
2 Musical Pub Crawl
3 Literary Pub Crawl
4 1916 Rebellion Walking Tour
5 Pat Liddy's Walking Tours
6 Viking Splash Tours
7 Trinity College Tour
8 City of a Thousand Welcomes

PATRICK ST.

ST. PATRICK'S CATHEDRAL

GOLDEN LN.

PETER ST.

PETER ROW

AUNGIER ST.

KEVIN ST. UPPER

BISHOP ST.

KEVIN ST. LOWER

MILL ST.

150 Meters
150 Yards

LWR. YORK ST.

UPR. MERCER ST.

GAIETY THEATRE

KING ST.

MERCER ST.

GLOVERS ALLEY

WEST

CUFFE ST.

LUAS TRAM GREEN LINE →

---

branch of the National Museum is itself a national treasure.

Under one dome, it's wonderfully digestible. Ireland's Bronze Age gold fills the center. Up four steps, a prehistoric Ireland exhibit rings the gold. In a corner (behind a 2,000-year-old body), you'll find the treasury, with the museum's most famous pieces (brooches, chalices, and other examples of Celtic metalwork). The collection's superstar is the gold, enamel, and amber eighth-century Tara Brooch. The best Viking artifacts in town are upstairs with the medieval collection. If you'll be visit-

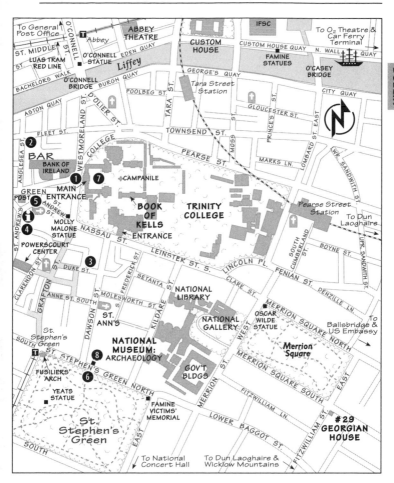

ing Cong (in Connemara, near Galway), seek out the original Cross of Cong.

Cost and Hours: Free, Tue-Sat 10:00-17:00, Sun 14:00-17:00, closed Mon, good café, between Trinity College and St. Stephen's Green on Kildare Street, tel. 01/677-7444—call in morning for sporadic tour schedule, www.museum.ie..

Nearby: As you exit the museum, glance over at **Leinster House,** next door (guarded and safely distant from the street). It was once the Duke of Leinster's town residence. Today, it houses the Irish Dail (parliament) and Seanad (senate), which meet here 90 days of each year.

▲**National Gallery**—This museum has Ireland's best collection of European masters: Vermeer, Caravaggio, Monet, and Picasso. It also features a hall that displays the work of top Irish painters, including Jack Yeats (the brother of the famous poet). It's impressive—although not nearly as extensive as national galleries in London or Paris. Study the floor-plan flier and take advantage of the free audioguide. Be sure to walk the series of rooms on the ground floor devoted to Irish painting and get to know artists you may never have heard of before. Visit the National Portrait Gallery on the mezzanine level for an insight into the great personalities of Ireland. You'll find Caravaggio and Vermeer on the top floor. In his *Taking of Christ*, Caravaggio, master of the chiaroscuro style, makes dramatic use of light and shadow for emphasis. Vermeer's *Lady Writing a Letter with her Maid*, one of only 30-some known works by the Dutch artist, shows his trademark focus on life's quiet moments.

Cost and Hours: Free, Mon-Sat 9:30-17:30, Thu until 20:30, Sun 12:00-17:30, Merrion Square West, tel. 01/661-5133, www.nationalgallery.ie.

Tours: The museum offers free audioguide tours (donations accepted) and free 45-minute guided tours (Sat at 14:00, Sun at 13:00 and 14:00).

National Library—Literature holds a lofty place in the Irish psyche. To feel the fire-and-ice pulse of Ireland's most famous literary greats, visit the annually changing exhibits in the library basement. The exhibits flesh out the very human passions of these writers, with samples of handwritten manuscripts and surprisingly interesting mini-documentaries of the times they lived in. Upstairs, you can get help making use of the library records to trace your genealogy.

Cost and Hours: Free, Mon-Wed 9:30-21:00, Thu-Fri 9:30-17:00, Sat 9:30-16:30, closed Sun, tel. 01/603-0277, 2-3 Kildare Street, www.nli.ie.

Merrion Square and Nearby

▲**Merrion Square**—Laid out in 1762, this square is ringed by elegant Georgian houses decorated with fine doors, a Dublin trademark. (If you're inspired by the ornate knobs and knockers, there's a shop by that name on nearby Nassau Street.) The park, once the exclusive domain of the residents, is now a delightful public escape and ideal for a picnic. To learn what "snogging" is, walk through the park on a sunny day, when it's full of smooching lovers. Oscar Wilde, lounging wittily on a boulder on the corner nearest the town center and surrounded by his clever quotes, provides a fun photo op.

▲▲**Number Twenty-Nine Georgian**

House—The carefully restored house at Number 29 Lower Fitzwilliam Street gives an intimate glimpse of middle-class Georgian life (which seems pretty high-class). From the side-walk, descend the stairs to the basement-level entrance (corner of Lower Fitzwilliam and Lower Mount Streets, opposite southern corner of Merrion Square). Start with an interesting 15-minute video (you're welcome to bring in a cup of coffee from the café) before joining your guide, who takes you on a fascinating 35-minute walk through this 1790 Dublin home.

Cost and Hours: €6, tours leave regularly, Tue-Sat 10:00-17:00, Sun 12:00-17:00, closed Mon, tel. 01/702-6165.

Grafton Street and St. Stephen's Green

▲▲**Grafton Street**—Once filled with noisy traffic, today's Grafton Street is Dublin's liveliest pedestrian shopping mall and people-watching paradise. A 10-minute stroll past street musicians takes you from Trinity College to St. Stephen's Green (and makes you wonder why some American merchants are so terrified of a car-free street). Walking south from Trinity College, you'll pass a buxom statue of "sweet" Molly Malone (also known as "the tart with the cart"). Next, you'll pass two venerable department stores: the Irish Brown Thomas and the English Marks & Spencer. Johnson's Court alley leads to the Powerscourt Townhouse Shopping Centre, which tastefully fills a converted Georgian mansion. The huge, glass-covered St. Stephen's Green Shopping Centre and the peaceful green itself mark the top of Grafton Street. For fun, gather a pile of coins and walk the street, putting each human statue into action with a donation. Consider stopping at the recommended Bewley's Café for coffee with a second-floor view of the action.

▲**St. Stephen's Green**—This city park was originally a medieval commons, complete with gory public executions. It was enclosed in 1664 and gradually surrounded with fine Georgian buildings. Today, it provides 22 acres of grassy refuge for Dubliners. At the northwest corner (near the end of Grafton Street) you'll be confronted by a looming marble arch erected to honor British officers killed during the Boer War. Locals nicknamed it "Traitor's Arch," as most Irish sympathized with the underdog Boers. On a sunny afternoon, this open space is a wonderful world apart from the big city. When marveling at the elegance of Georgian Dublin, remember that during the Georgian period, Dublin was the second-most important city in the British Empire. Area big shots knew that any money wrung from the local populace not spent in Dublin would end up in London. Since it was "use it or lose it," they used it—with gusto—to beautify their city.

Dublin Castle and Nearby

▲▲**Dublin Castle**—Built on the spot of the first Viking fortress, this castle was the seat of English rule in Ireland for 700 years. Located where the Poddle and Liffey rivers came together, making a black pool (*dubh linn* in Irish), Dublin Castle was the official residence of the viceroy who implemented the will of the British royalty. In this stirring setting, the Brits handed power over to Michael Collins and the Irish in 1922. Today, it's used for fancy state and charity functions.

Standing in the courtyard, you can imagine the ugliness of the British-Irish situation. Notice the statue of justice above the gate—pointedly without her blindfold and admiring her sword. As Dubliners say, "There she stands, above her station, with her face to the palace and her arse to the nation." The fancy interior is viewable only with a 45-minute tour, which offers a fairly boring room-by-room walk through the lavish state apartments of this most English of Irish palaces. The tour finishes with a look at the foundations of the Norman tower and the best remaining chunk of the 13th-century town wall.

Cost and Hours: €4.50, buy tickets in courtyard under portico opposite clock tower, required tours depart hourly, Mon-Sat 10:00-16:45, Sun 12:00-16:45, tel. 01/677-7129, www.dublin castle.ie.

▲▲**Chester Beatty Library**—Chester Beatty was a rich American mining engineer who retired to Ireland in 1950, later becoming its first honorary citizen. He left this priceless and eclectic collection to his adopted homeland as a public charitable trust. Today, Ireland has put a modern glass roof over the parade ground separating two old army barracks and filled it with Beatty's treasures. It's a small collection, but delightfully displayed and described. The top floor focuses on the world's great religions (strong on Islam and Christianity) with displays on dervish whirls, calligraphy in Islam, and early Asian Christian manuscripts. The bottom floor is all about the written word, with topics including etching, medieval bookbinding, and fine old manuscripts.

As you wander, you'll see books carved out of jade, ornate snuff bottles, rhino-horn cups, and even the oldest surviving copy of St. Paul's letter to the Romans (A.D. 180). Other highlights include a graceful Burmese book written on palm leaves—bound together to unfold like an accordion—and a densely ornamental sunburst motif from a 500-year-old Iranian Quran.

Cost and Hours: Free; May–Sept Mon-Fri 10:00-17:00, Sat 11:00-17:00, Sun 13:00-17:00; Oct–April Tue-Fri 10:00-17:00, Sat 11:00-17:00, Sun 13:00-17:00, closed Mon; coffee shop, tel. 01/407-0750, www.cbl.ie). You'll find the library behind Dublin Castle (follow the signs).

Dublin City Hall—The first Georgian building in this very Georgian city stands proudly overlooking Dame Street, in front of the gate to Dublin Castle. Built in 1779 as the Royal Exchange, it introduced the Georgian style (then very popular in Britain and on the Continent) to Ireland. Step inside (it's free) to feel the prosperity and confidence of Dublin in her 18th-century glory days. In 1852, this building became the City Hall. Under the grand rotunda, a cycle of heroic paintings tells the city's history. (The mosaics on the floor convey such homilies as "Obedience makes the happiest citizenry.")

Pay your respects to the 18-foot-tall statue of Daniel O'Connell, the great orator and liberator who, in 1829, won emancipation for Catholics in Ireland from the much-despised Protestants over in London. The body of modern Irish rebel leader Michael Collins lay in state here after his assassination in 1922. The greeter sits like the Maytag repairman at the information desk, eager to give you more information. Downstairs is the excellent *Story of the Capital* exhibition, which has storyboards and video clips of Dublin's history.

Cost and Hours: €4, free audioguide, coffee shop, Mon-Sat 10:00-17:00, closed Sun, tel. 01/222-2204, www.dublincity.ie.

Dublin's Cathedrals Area

Because of Dublin's English past (particularly Henry VIII's Reformation, which led to the dissolution of the Catholic monasteries in 1539—in Ireland as well as England), neither of its top two churches is Catholic. Christ Church Cathedral and nearby St. Patrick's Cathedral are both Church of Ireland (Anglican). In the late 19th century, the cathedrals underwent extensive restoration. The rich Guinness brewery family forked out the dough to try to make St. Patrick's Cathedral outshine Christ Church—whose patrons were the equally rich, rival Jameson family of distillery fame. However, in Catholic Ireland, these Anglican sights feel hollow, and they're more famous than visit-worthy.

Christ Church Cathedral—Occupying the same site as the first wooden church built on this spot by King Sitric in Viking times (c. 1040), the present structure dates from a mix of periods: Norman and Gothic, but mostly Victorian Neo-Gothic (1870s restoration work). Inside you'll find the reputed tomb of the Norman warlord Strongbow, who led the thin edge of the English military wedge that eventually dominated Ireland for centuries. This oldest building in Dublin has an unusually large underground crypt, containing stocks, statues, and the cathedral's silver.

Cost and Hours: €6 donation to church includes downstairs crypt silver exhibition, €12.25 combo-ticket includes Dublinia (described next)—saving you €1.25; Mon-Sat 9:30-18:30, Sun 12:30-14:30, free brochure with self-guided tour, tel. 01/677-8099, http://cccdub.ie.

Evensong: A 45-minute evensong service is sung several times a week (Wed, Sat, and Sun at 18:00; less often in summer).

▲**Dublinia**—This exhibit, which highlights Dublin's Viking and medieval past, is a hit with youngsters. Beefed up during a 2010 renovation, the exhibits are laid out on three floors. The ground floor focuses on Viking Dublin, explaining life aboard a Viking ship and inside a Viking house. Viking traders introduced urban life and commerce to Ireland—but kids will be most interested in gawking at their gory weaponry.

The next floor up reveals Dublin's day-to-day life in medieval times, from chivalrous knights and damsels in town fairs to the brutal ravages of the Plague. The huge scale model of medieval Dublin is especially well done. The top floor's "History Hunters" section is devoted to how the puzzles of modern archaeology and science shed light on Dublin's history. From this floor you can climb a couple of flights of stairs into the tower for so-so views of Dublin, or exit across an enclosed stone bridge to adjacent Christ Church Cathedral.

Cost and Hours: €7.50, €12.25 combo-ticket includes Christ Church Cathedral; daily March-Sept 10:00-17:00, Oct-Feb 11:00-16:30, last entry 45 minutes before closing, top-floor coffee shop open in summer, across from Christ Church Cathedral, tel. 01/679-4611, www.dublinia.ie.

St. Patrick's Cathedral—The first church here was built on the site where St. Patrick baptized local pagan converts. The core of the Gothic structure you see today was built in the 13th century. After the Reformation, it passed into the hands of the Anglican Church. A century later, Oliver Cromwell's puritanical Calvinist troops—who considered the Anglicans to be little more than Catholics without a pope—stabled their horses here as a sign of disrespect.

Jonathan Swift (author of *Gulliver's Travels*) was dean of the Cathedral for 32 years in the 18th century. His grave is located near the front door (on the right side of the nave), where his cutting, self-penned epitaph reads: "He lies where furious indignation can no longer rend his heart." Check out the large wooden Door of Reconciliation hanging in the north transept, with the rough hole in the middle. This was the Chapter House door through which two feuding, sword-bearing 15th-century nobles shook hands..."chancing their arms" and giving the Irish that expression of trust.

Cost and Hours: €5.50 donation to church; Mon-Sat 9:00-17:00, Sun 12:30-14:30, last entry one hour before closing.

Evensong: Mon-Fri at 17:45, Sun at 15:15, none Wed July-Aug.

▲▲Temple Bar

Three hundred years ago, this was the city waterfront, where tall sailing ships offloaded their goods (a "bar" was a loading dock

along the river, and the Temples were a dominant merchant family). Eventually, the city grew eastward, filling in tidal mudflats, to create the docklands of modern Dublin. Once a thriving Georgian center of craftsmen and merchants, this neighborhood fell on hard times in the 19th century. Ensuing low rents attracted students and artists, giving the area a bohemian flair. With government tax incentives and lots of development money, the Temple Bar district has now become a thriving cultural (and beer-drinking) hot spot. This much-promoted center—with trendy shops, cafés, theaters, galleries, pubs with live music, and restaurants—feels like the heart of the city. It's Dublin's "Left Bank," and like in Paris, it's on the south shore of the river. It fills the cobbled streets between Dame Street and the River Liffey.

Temple Bar is an absolute spectacle in the evening, when it bursts with revelers. The noise, pushy crowds, and inflated prices have driven most Dubliners away. But even if you're just gawking, don't miss the opportunity to wander through this human circus. It can be a real zoo on summer weekend nights, holidays, and nights after big sporting events let out. Women in funky hats, part of loud "hen" (bachelorette) parties, promenade down the main drag as drunken dudes shout from pub doorways to get their attention. Be aware that a pint of beer here is €6—about €1 more than at less-glitzy pubs just a couple of blocks away (north of the River Liffey or south of Dame Street).

Temple Bar Square, just off Temple Bar Street (near Ha' Penny Bridge), is the epicenter of activity. It hosts free street theater and a Saturday book market, and has handy ATMs. On busy weekends, people-watching here is a contact sport. You're bound to meet some characters.

Irish music fans find great CDs at **Claddagh Records** (Cecilia Street, just around the corner from Luigi Malone's, Mon and Wed-Sat 11:30-17:30, closed Sun and Tue). Unlike big, glitzy chain stores, this is a little hole-in-the-wall shop staffed by informed folks who love turning visitors on to Irish tunes. Grab a couple of

CDs for your drive through the Irish countryside. Farther west and somewhat hidden is **Meeting House Square,** with a lively organic-produce market (Sat 10:00-18:00). Bordering the square is the **Irish Film Institute** (main entry on Eustace Street), which shows a variety of art-house flicks. A bohemian crowd relaxes in its bar/café, awaiting the next film (6 Eustace Street, box office daily 13:30-21:00, tel. 01/679-5744, www.irishfilm.ie).

Rather than follow particular pub or restaurant recommendations (mine are listed later, under "Eating in Dublin"), venture down a few side lanes off the main drag to see what looks good.

The pedestrian-only **Ha' Penny Bridge,** named for the halfpence toll people used to pay to cross it, leads from Temple Bar over the River Liffey to the opposite bank and more sights. If the rowdy Temple Bar scene gets too much, cross over to the north bank of the River Liffey on the Millennium Pedestrian Bridge (next bridge west of the Ha' Penny Bridge), where you'll find a mellower, more cosmopolitan choice of restaurants with outdoor seating in the Millennium Walk district.

North of the River Liffey
▲▲O'Connell Bridge

This bridge spans the River Liffey, which has historically divided the wealthy, cultivated south side of town from the poorer, cruder north side. While there's plenty of culture north of the river, even today "the north" is considered rougher and less safe. Dubliners joke that north-side residents are known as "the accused," while residents on the south side are addressed as "your honor."

From the bridge, look upriver (west) as far upstream as you can see. On the left in the distance, the **big concrete building**—considered an eyesore by locals—houses the city planning commission, which, ironically, is in charge of making sure new buildings are built in good taste. It squats on the still-buried precious artifacts of the first Viking settlement, established in Dublin in the ninth century.

Across the river stands the **Four Courts**—the Supreme Court building. It was shelled and burned in 1922, during the tragic civil war that followed Irish independence. The national archives office burned, and irreplaceable birth records were lost, making it more difficult today for those with Irish roots to trace their ancestry. The closest bridge upstream—the elegant iron **Ha' Penny Bridge** (see photo above)—leads left, into the Temple Bar nightlife district. Just beyond that old-fashioned, 19th-century bridge is Dublin's pedestrian **Millennium Bridge,** inaugurated in 2000. (Note that buses leave from O'Connell Bridge—specifically Aston Quay—for the Guinness Storehouse and Kilmainham Gaol.)

Turn 180 degrees and look downstream to see the tall **Liberty Hall** union headquarters—for now, the tallest building in the Republic (16 stories tall, some say in honor of the 1916 Easter Uprising)—and lots of cranes. Modern Dublin is developing downstream. The Irish (forever clever tax fiddlers) have subsidized and revitalized this formerly dreary quarter with great success. A short walk downstream along the north bank leads to a powerful series of gaunt statues memorializing the Great Potato Famine of 1845-1849. Beyond, you'll see the masts of the *Jeanie Johnston*, a replica transport ship.

▲▲O'Connell Street Stroll

Dublin's grandest street leads from O'Connell Bridge through the heart of north Dublin. Since the 1740s, it has been a 45-yard-wide promenade, and ever since the first O'Connell Bridge connected it to the Trinity side of town in 1794, it's been Dublin's main drag. (However, it was only named O'Connell after independence was won in 1922.) These days, the city has made the street more pedestrian-friendly, and a new LUAS line extension will eventually run within the median. Though lined with fast-food and souvenir shops, O'Connell Street echoes with history.

• *Take the following stroll along the wide, tree-lined median strip, which is less crowded than either sidewalk, and closer to the statues I mention here. Start at the base of the street, near O'Connell Bridge.*

Statues and Monuments: The median running down the middle of O'Connell Street is lined with statues celebrating great figures from Ireland's past. At the base of the street stands **Daniel O'Connell** (1775-1847), known as "the Liberator" for founding the Catholic Association and demanding Irish Catholic rights in the British Parliament.

Walk a block east down Abbey Street to find the famous **Abbey Theatre**— rebuilt after a fire into a nondescript, modern building. It's still the much-loved home of the Irish National Theatre.

The statue of **James Larkin** honors the founder of the Irish Transport Workers' Union. The one monument that didn't wave an Irish flag—a tall column crowned by a statue of the British hero of Trafalgar, Admiral Horatio Nelson—was blown up in 1966...the IRA's contribution to the local celebration of the Easter

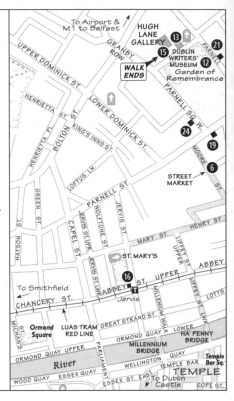

1. Daniel O'Connell Statue
2. Abbey Theatre
3. James Larkin Statue
4. Millennium Spire
5. General Post Office
6. Moore Street Market
7. St. Mary's Pro-Cathedral
8. Father Matthew Statue
9. Gresham Hotel
10. Charles Stewart Parnell Monument
11. Gate Theatre
12. Garden of Remembrance
13. Dublin Writers' Museum
14. James Joyce Cultural Ctr.
15. The Hugh Lane Gallery & Francis Bacon Studio
16. National Leprechaun Museum

Accommodations & Services

17. Jurys Inn Custom House
18. The Townhouse
19. Jurys Inn Parnell Street
20. Belvedere Hotel
21. Charles Stewart Hotel
22. Internet Café
23. Bike Tours
24. Rebel Tours

Uprising's 50th anniversary.

This spot is now occupied by the 390-foot-tall, stainless steel **Millennium Spire** that was finally completed in 2003. While it trumpets rejuvenation on that side of the river, it's a memorial to nothing and has no real meaning. Dubious Dubliners call it the tallest waste of €5 million in all of Europe. Its nickname? Take your pick: the Stiletto in the Ghetto, the Stiffy on the Liffey, the Pole in the Hole, the Poker near the Croker (after nearby Croke Park), or the Spike in the Dike.

• *On your left is the...*

General Post Office: This is not just any P.O. It was from here that Patrick Pearse read the Proclamation of Irish Independence in 1916, kicking off the Easter Uprising. The G.P.O. building itself—a kind of Irish Alamo—was the rebel headquarters and scene of a bloody five-day siege that followed the proclama-

tion. Its pillars remain pockmarked with bullet holes (open for business and sightseers Mon-Sat 8:00-20:00, closed Sun).

Tucked in the ground floor of the building is the small **An Post Museum,** which stamp collectors and Irish rebels at heart will enjoy (€2, Mon-Fri 10:00-17:00, Sat 10:00-16:00, closed Sun, on the right as you enter, www.anpost.ie/historyandheritage).

• *Turn left (west) past the post office, down people-filled Henry Street (residents' favorite shopping lane), then wander to the right into the nearby...*

Moore Street Market: Many of its merchants have staffed the same stalls for decades. Start a conversation. It's a great worka-day scene. You'll see lots of mums with strollers—a reminder that Ireland is one of Europe's youngest countries, with more than 35 percent of the population under the age of 25 (Mon-Sat 8:00-18:00, closed Sun).

• *Back on O'Connell Street, return to the median strip and continue your walk. A block east (right) of O'Connell, down Cathedral Street, is...*

St. Mary's Pro-Cathedral: Although this is Dublin's leading

Modern Ireland's Turbulent Birth: A Timeline

Imagine if our American patriot ancestors had fought both our Revolutionary War and our Civil War over a span of seven chaotic years...and then appreciate the remarkable resilience of the Irish people. Here's a summary of what happened when.

1916: A nationalist militia called the Volunteers (led by **Patrick Pearse**) and the socialist Irish Citizen Army (led by **James Connolly**) join forces in the **Easter Uprising,** but they fail to end 750 years of British rule. The uprising is unpopular with most Irish, who are unhappy with the destruction in Dublin and preoccupied with the "Great War" on the Continent. But when 16 rebel leaders (including Pearse and Connolly) are executed, Irish public opinion reverses as sympathy grows for the martyrs and the cause of Irish Independence.

Two important rebel leaders escape execution. New York-born **Eamon de Valera** is spared because of his American passport (the British don't want to anger their potential ally in World War I). **Michael Collins,** a low-ranking rebel officer who fought in the uprising at the General Post Office, refines urban guerrilla-warfare strategies in prison, then blossoms after his release as the rebels' military and intelligence leader in the power vacuum that followed the executions.

1918: World War I ends, and a general election is held in Ireland. Outside of Ulster, the nationalist **Sinn Fein** party wins 73 out of 79 seats in Parliament. Only 4 out of 32 counties vote to maintain the Union with Britain (all 4 are in Ulster, part of which would become Northern Ireland). Rather than take their seats in London, Sinn Fein representatives abstain from participating in a government they see as foreign occupiers.

1919: On January 19, the abstaining Sinn Fein members set up a rebel government in

Catholic church, it rather curiously isn't a "cathedral." The pope declared Christ Church to be a cathedral in the 12th century—and later, gave St. Patrick's the same designation. (The Vatican has chosen to stubbornly ignore the fact that Christ Church and St. Patrick's haven't been Catholic for centuries.) Completed in 1821, this church is done in the style of a Greek temple.

• *Continuing up O'Connell Street, you'll find a statue of...*

Father Matthew: A leader of the temperance movement of the 1830s, some historians claim Father Matthew was responsible for enough Irish peasants staying sober to enable Daniel

Dublin called Dail Eireann. On the same day, the first shots of the **Irish War of Independence** are fired as rebels begin ambushing police barracks, which are seen as an extension of British rule. De Valera is elected by the Dail to lead the rebels, with Collins as his deputy. Collins' web of spies infiltrates British intelligence at Dublin Castle. The Volunteers rename themselves the **Irish Republican Army;** meanwhile the British beef up their military presence in Ireland by sending in tough WWI vets, the Black and Tans. A bloody and very personal war ensues.

1921: Having lived through the slaughter of World War I, the British tire of the extended bloodshed in Ireland and begin negotiations with the rebels. De Valera leads rebel negotiations, but then entrusts them to Collins (a clever politician, De Valera sees that whoever signs a treaty will be blamed for its compromises). Understanding the tricky position he's been placed in, Collins signs the **Anglo-Irish Treaty** in December, lamenting that in doing so he has signed his "own death warrant."

The Dail narrowly ratifies the treaty (64 to 57), but Collins' followers are unable to convince De Valera's supporters that the compromises are a stepping stone to later full independence. De Valera and his anti-treaty disciples resign in protest. **Arthur Griffith,** founder of Sinn Fein, assumes the presidential post.

In June, the anti-treaty forces, holed up in the Four Courts building, are fired upon by Collins and his pro-treaty forces—thus igniting the **Irish Civil War.** The British want the treaty to stand and even supply Collins with cannons, meanwhile threatening to re-enter Ireland if the anti-treaty forces aren't put down.

1922: In August, Griffith dies of stress-induced illness, and Collins is assassinated 10 days later. Nevertheless, the pro-treaty forces prevail, as they are backed by popular opinion and better (British-supplied) military equipment.

1923: In April, the remaining IRA forces dump (or stash) their arms, ending the civil war...but many of their bitter vets vow to carry on the fight. De Valera distances himself from the IRA and becomes the dominant Irish political leader for the next 40 years.

O'Connell to organize them into a political force. (Perhaps studying this example, the USSR was careful to keep the price of vodka affordable.)

Nearby, the fancy **Gresham Hotel** is a good place for an elegant tea or beer. In an earlier era, this was where the beautiful people would alight during visits to Dublin. In the 1960s, Richard Burton and Liz Taylor stayed here while he was filming *The Spy Who Came in from the Cold.* (In those days, parts of Dublin were drab enough to pass for an inaccessible Eastern Bloc city.)

• *Standing boldly at the top of O'Connell Street is a monument to...*

Charles Stewart Parnell
(1846-1891)

Parnell, who led the Irish movement for Home Rule in the 1880s, served time in Kilmainham Gaol. A Cambridge-educated Protestant of landed-gentry stock and a member of Parliament, he had a vision of a modern and free Irish nation filled mostly with Catholics but not set up as a religious state. Despite his privileged birth, Parnell gained the love of the Irish people—who remembered their grandparents' harsh evictions during the famine—through his tireless work on land reforms to secure fair rents and land tenure. Momentum seemed to be on his side. With the British prime minister of the time, William Gladstone, in favor of a similar form of Home Rule, it looked as if all of Ireland was ripe for independence, as a Commonwealth nation similar to Canada or Australia. Then a sex scandal broke around Parnell and his mistress, the wife of another Parliament member. The press, egged on by the powerful Catholic bishops (who didn't want a secular, free Irish state), battered away at the scandal until finally Parnell was driven from office. Sadly, after that, Ireland became mired in the Troubles of the 20th century: an awkward independence (1921) featuring a divided island, a bloody civil war, and sectarian violence ever since. Wracked with exhaustion and only in his mid-40s, Parnell is thought to have died of a broken heart.

Charles Stewart Parnell: The names of the four ancient provinces of Ireland and all 32 Irish counties (North *and* South, since this was erected before Irish independence) ring the monument, honoring Charles Stewart Parnell, the member of Parliament who nearly won Home Rule for Ireland in the late 1800s. (A sex scandal cost Parnell the support of the Church, which let the air out of the movement for a free Ireland.)

• *Continue straight up Parnell Square East. At the* **Gate Theatre** *(on the left), Orson Welles and James Mason had their professional acting debuts. One block up on the left is the...*

Garden of Remembrance: Honoring the victims of the 1916 Uprising, the park was dedicated in 1966 on the 50th anniversary of the revolt that ultimately led to Irish independence. The bottom of the cross-shaped pool is a mosaic of Celtic weapons, symbolic of how the early Irish would proclaim peace by breaking their

Dublin's Literary Life

Dublin in the 1700s, grown rich from a lucrative cloth trade, was one of Europe's most cultured and sophisticated cities.

The buildings were decorated in the Georgian style still visible today, and the city's Protestant elite shuttled between here and London, bridging the Anglo-Irish cultural gap. Jonathan Swift (1667-1745), the great satirical writer, was also dean of St. Patrick's Cathedral (1713-1745) and one of the city's eminent citizens. Then, around the turn of the 20th century, Dublin produced some of the world's great modern writers: Bram Stoker (1847-1912), Oscar Wilde (1854-1900), George Bernard Shaw (1856-1950), William Butler Yeats (1865-1939), and James Joyce (1882-1941), to name just a few.

weapons and throwing them into a lake or river. The Irish flag flies above the park: green for Catholics, orange for Protestants, and white for the hope that they can live together in peace.

One of modern Ireland's most stirring moments occurred here in May of 2011, when Queen Elizabeth II made this the first stop on her historic visit to Ireland. She laid a wreath at the Children of Lir sculpture under this flag, and bowed her head for a moment of silence out of respect for the Irish rebels who had fought and died trying to gain freedom from her United Kingdom...a hugely cathartic moment

for both nations. Until this visit, no British monarch had set foot in the Irish state since its founding 90 years earlier (free, daily 8:30-18:00).

• *On the uphill side, across the street, is a splendidly restored Georgian mansion, housing the...*

Dublin Writers' Museum: No other country so small has produced such a wealth of literature. As interesting to fans of Irish literature as it is boring to those who aren't, this three-room museum features the lives and works of Dublin's great writers (€7.50, includes helpful audioguide, ask about €11.50

combo-ticket with James Joyce Museum in Dun Laoghaire; Mon-Sat 10:00-17:00, Sun 11:00-17:00, June-Aug Mon-Fri until 18:00; coffee shop, 18 Parnell Square North, tel. 01/872-2077, www .writersmuseum.com).

With hometown wits such as Swift, Stoker, Yeats, Joyce, Wilde, and Shaw, Dublin has a checklist of residences and memorials to see. Aficionados of James Joyce's work may want to hike two blocks east to visit the **James Joyce Cultural Centre** (€5; June-Aug Tue-Sat 10:00-17:00, Sun 12:00-17:00, closed Mon; Sept-May closed Sun-Mon; 35 North Great George's Street, tel. 01/878-8547). There's more Joyce memorabilia in Dun Laoghaire at the **James Joyce Museum**.

• *Next door to the Dublin Writers' Museum is...*

The Hugh Lane Gallery: In a grand Neoclassical building, this has a fine, bite-size selection of Pre-Raphaelite, French Impressionist, and 19th- and 20th-century Irish paintings. Sir Hugh went down on the *Lusitania* in 1915; due to an unclear will, his collection is shared by this gallery and the National Gallery in London.

Tucked in the back of the gallery is the **Francis Bacon Studio,** reconstructed here in its original (messy) state from its London location at the time of the artist's death in 1992. Born in Dublin and inspired by Pablo Picasso, Bacon's shocking paintings reflected his belief that "chaos breeds energy." This compact space contains touch-screen terminals, display cases of personal items, and a few unfinished works. The 10-minute film interview of Bacon may fascinate like-minded viewers...and disquiet others (free, Tue-Thu 10:00-18:00, Fri-Sat 10:00-17:00, Sun 11:00-17:00, closed Mon, tel. 01/222-5564, www.hughlane.ie). Check out their free Sundays@Noon classical music concerts (Oct-June).

• *Your walk is over. Here on the north end of town, it's convenient to visit the Gaelic Athletic Association Museum at Croke Park Stadium (a 20-minute walk or short taxi ride away). Otherwise, hop on your skateboard and zip back to the river.*

More Sights North of the River Liffey

National Leprechaun Museum—This good-natured, low-tech attraction is fine for kids and lighthearted adults (but too corny for teens). An uninhibited guide leads the group on a 45-minute meander through Irish mythology. You'll visit a wishing well, a giant's living room, and a fairy fort listening to tales that will enchant your wee ones.

Cost and Hours: €10, Mon-Sat 9:30-18:30, Sun 10:30-18:30, last entry 45 minutes before closing, a block north of the River Liffey on Abbey Street across from Jervis LUAS stop, tel. 01/873-

3899, www.leprechaunmuseum.ie.

The *Jeanie Johnston* (Tall Ship Famine Museum)—This modern seaworthy replica of a transport ship, docked on the River Liffey, is modeled after its namesake. The original *Jeanie Johnston* embarked on 16 six- to eight- week transatlantic crossings, carrying more than 2,500 Irish emigrants to their new lives in America and Canada the decade after the Great Potato Famine. While many barely seaworthy hulks were known as "coffin ships," those who boarded the *Jeanie Johnston* were lucky: With a humanitarian captain and even a doctor, not one life was lost. Your tour guide will introduce you to the ship's main characters and help illuminate day-to-day life aboard a cramped tall ship 150 years ago. Because this ship makes goodwill voyages to Atlantic ports, it may be away during your visit.

Cost and Hours: €8.50, visits by 45-minute tour only, hourly April-Oct 11:00-16:00, Nov-March 11:00-15:00, on the north bank of the Liffey just east of Sean O'Casey Bridge, tel. 01/473-0111, www.jeaniejohnston.ie.

Dublin's Smithfield Village

This neighborhood is worth a look for the Old Jameson Distillery whiskey tour and Dublin's most authentic traditional-music pub. The two sights are on a long square, two blocks northwest of the Four Courts—the Supreme Court building. The modern square still fulfills its original function as a horse market (first Sat mornings of the month, great for people-watching). The **Fresh Market,** near the top of the square, is a handy grocery stop for urban picnic fixings (Mon-Sat 7:00-22:00, Sun 8:00-22:00).

Old Jameson Distillery—Whiskey fans enjoy visiting the old distillery. You get a 10-minute video, a 20-minute tour, and a free shot in the pub. Unfortunately, the "distillery" feels fake and put together for tourists. The Bushmills tour in Northern Ireland (in a working factory) and the Midleton tour near Cork (in the huge original factory) are better experiences. If you do take this tour, volunteer energetically when offered the chance: This will get you a coveted seat at the whiskey taste-test table at the the tour's end.

Cost and Hours: €13.50, daily 9:30-18:30, last tour at 17:15, Bow Street, tel. 01/807-2355, www.jamesonwhiskey.com/ojd.

Evening Events: Jameson offers "Irish Nights"—a splurge dinner-and-dance shindig with all the trimmings (€50, includes guided tour, cocktail, and four-course meal—book ahead; April-Oct Thu-Sat at 19:00).

Cobblestone Pub—Hiding in a derelict-looking building at the top of the square, this pub offers Dublin's least glitzy and most rewarding traditional-music venue. The candlelit walls, covered with photos of honored trad musicians, set the tone. Music is revered here, as reflected in the understated sign: "Listening area, please respect musicians" (daily 17:00-23:45, trad-music sessions Mon-Wed at 21:00, Thu-Sat at 17:00, Sun at 14:00; at north end of square, 100 yards from Old Jameson Distillery's brick chimney tower; tel. 01/872-1799, www.cobblestonepub.ie).

Outer Dublin

The Kilmainham Gaol and the Guinness Storehouse are located to the west of the old center and can be combined in one visit (linked by a 20-minute walk or a five-minute taxi ride).

▲▲▲**Kilmainham Gaol (Jail)**—Opened in 1796 as both the

Dublin County Jail and a debtors' prison, it was considered a model in its day. In reality, this jail was frequently used by the British as a political prison. Many of those who fought for Irish independence were held or executed here, including leaders of the rebellions of 1798, 1803, 1848, 1867, and 1916.
National heroes Robert Emmett and Charles Stewart Parnell each did time here. The last prisoner to be held here was Eamon de Valera, who later became president of Ireland. He was released on July 16, 1924, the day Kilmainham was finally shut down. The buildings, virtually in ruins, were restored in the 1960s. Today, it's a shrine to the Nathan Hales of Ireland.

Start your visit with a one-hour guided **tour** (2/hour, includes 15-minute prison-history slide show in the prison chapel—spend waiting time in museum). It's touching to tour the cells and places of execution—hearing tales of terrible colonialism and heroic patriotism—alongside Irish schoolkids who know these names well. The museum is an excellent exhibit on Victorian prison life and Ireland's fight for independence. Don't miss the museum's dimly lit Last Words 1916 hall upstairs, which displays the stirring final letters that patriots sent to loved ones hours before facing the firing squad.

Cost and Hours: €6, daily 9:30-18:00, last entry one hour before closing, tel. 01/453-5984. The humble cafeteria serves little more than sandwiches.

Connecting the Gaol and Guinness Storehouse: To get from Aston Quay or the Guinness Storehouse to Kilmainham Gaol, you can take a taxi, or catch bus #51B, #69, #78A, or #79. Another option is to take one of the hop-on, hop-off buses: City Sightseeing Dublin stops right at Kilmainham Gaol, while Dublin Bus Tour stops 200 yards away, in front of the modern art

The Famous Record-Breaking Records Book

Look up "beer" in the *Guinness World Records* and you'll discover that the strongest one ever sold was a Scottish brew called *The End of History* (55 percent alcohol) and that a man set a record for removing beer bottle caps with his teeth (63 in one minute). But aside from listing records for amazing—or amazingly stupid—feats, this famous record book has a more subtle connection with beer.

In 1951, while hunting in Ireland's County Wexford, Sir Hugh Beaver, then the managing director at Guinness Breweries, got into a debate with his companions over which was the fastest game bird in Europe: the golden plover or the red grouse. That night at his estate, after scouring countless reference books, they were disappointed not to find a definitive answer.

Beaver realized that similar questions were likely being debated nightly across pubs in Ireland and Britain. So he hired twins Norris and Ross McWhirter, who ran a fact-finding agency in London, to compile a book of answers to various questions. They set up an office at 107 Fleet Street and began assembling the first edition of the book by contacting experts, such as astrophysicists, etymologists, virologists, and volcanologists. In 1955, the *Guinness Book of Records* (later renamed *Guinness World Records*) was published. By Christmas, it topped the British bestseller list.

In the beginning, entries mostly focused on facts about natural phenomena and animal oddities, but grew to include a wide variety of extreme human achievements. After more than a half-century of noting record-breaking traditions around the globe, the volume continues to answer a multitude of burning trivia questions, such as the wealthiest cat in the world, the largest burrito ever made, and the record time for peeling 50 pounds of onions (an event that likely caused a lot of tears).

The iconic books are now available in more than 100 countries and 26 languages, with more than 3.5 million copies sold annually. As the bestselling copyrighted book of all time, it even earns a record-breaking entry within its own pages.

museum in Kilmainham hospital. Both tours stop at the Guinness Storehouse.

To catch the city bus from the jail to the Guinness Storehouse, leave the prison and take three rights—crossing no streets—to the bus stop, and hop bus #51B or #78A.

▲**Guinness Storehouse**—A visit to the Guinness Storehouse is, for many, a pilgrimage. Arthur Guinness began brewing the renowned stout here in 1759 and by 1868, it was the biggest brewery in the world. Today, the sprawling place fills several city blocks.

Around the world, Guinness brews more than 10 million pints a day (their biggest brewery is actually in Lagos, Nigeria). Although the home of Ireland's national beer welcomes visitors (for a price) with a sprawling modern museum, there are no tours of the actual working brewery. The museum fills the old fermentation plant used from 1902 through 1988, which reopened in 2000 as a huge shrine to the tradition. Step into the middle of the ground floor and look up. A tall, beer-glass-shaped glass atrium—14 million pints big—soars upward past four floors of exhibitions and cafés to the skylight. As you look down at Arthur's original 9,000-year lease, enshrined under glass in the floor...you realize that at £45 per year, it's been quite a bargain. Atop the building, the **Gravity Bar** provides visitors with a commanding 360-degree view of Dublin—with vistas all the way to the sea—and a free beer.

The actual exhibit makes brewing seem more grandiose than it is and treats Arthur like the god of human happiness. Highlights are the cooperage (with 1954 film clips showing the master wood-keg-makers plying their now virtually extinct trade), a display of the brewery's clever ads, and a small exhibit about the beer's connection to the *Guinness World Records* (see sidebar on previous page).

Cost and Hours: €15, includes a €5 pint; €1 off with your hop-on, hop-off bus ticket or 10 percent discount when booked online; daily 9:30-17:00, July-Aug until 19:00; enter on Bellevue Street, bus #78A from Aston Quay near O'Connell Bridge, or bus #123 from Dame Street and O'Connell Street; tel. 01/408-4800, www.guinness-storehouse.com. Both hop-on, hop-off bus tours also stop here.

▲**National Museum: Decorative Arts and History**—This branch of the National Museum, which occupies the huge, 18th-century stone Collins Barracks in west Dublin, displays Irish dress, furniture, weapons, silver, and other domestic baubles from the past 700 years. History buffs will linger longest in the "Soldiers & Chiefs" exhibit, which covers the Irish at war both at home and abroad since 1500 (including the American Civil War). The sober finale is the "Understanding 1916" room, offering Ireland's best coverage of its the painful birth of this nation, an event known as the "Terrible Beauty." Guns, personal letters, and death masks help illustrate the 1916 Easter Uprising, War of Independence against Britain, and Ireland's civil war. Croppies

Acre, the large park between the museum and the river, was the site of Dublin's largest soup kitchen during the Great Potato Famine in 1845-1849.

Cost and Hours: Free, Tue-Sat 10:00-17:00, Sun 14:00-17:00, closed Mon, good café; on north side of the River Liffey in Collins Barracks on Benburb Street, roughly across the river from Guinness Storehouse, easy to reach by LUAS—get off at Museum stop; tel. 01/648-6453, www.museum.ie. Call ahead for sporadic tour times.

▲**Gaelic Athletic Association Museum**—The GAA was founded in 1884 as an expression of an Irish cultural awakening (see sidebar, next page). It was created to foster the development of Gaelic sports, specifically Gaelic football and hurling, and to exclude English sports such as cricket and rugby. The GAA played an important part in the fight for independence. This museum, at 82,000-seat Croke Park Stadium in east Dublin (a 20-minute walk northeast of Parnell Square), offers a high-tech, interactive introduction to Ireland's favorite games. Relive the greatest moments in hurling and Irish-football history. Then get involved: Pick up a stick and try hurling, kick a football, and test your speed and balance. A 15-minute film (played on request) gives you a "Sunday at the stadium" experience.

Cost and Hours: €6; July-Aug daily 9:30-18:00; Sept-June Mon-Sat 9:30-17:00, Sun 12:00-17:00; on game Sundays the museum is open to ticket-holders only; located under the stands at Croke Park Stadium—enter from St. Joseph's Avenue off Clonliffe Road; tel. 01/819-2323, www.crokepark.ie/gaa-museum.

Tours: The €15, one-hour museum-plus-stadium-tour option is worth it only for rabid fans who want a glimpse of the huge stadium and yearn to know which locker room is considered the unlucky one.

Hurling or Gaelic Football at Croke Park Stadium—Actually seeing a match here, surrounded by incredibly spirited Irish fans, is a fun experience. Hurling is like airborne hockey with no injury time-outs. Gaelic football resembles a rugged form of soccer; you can carry the ball, but must bounce or kick it every three steps. Matches are held most Saturday or Sunday afternoons in summer (May-Aug), culminating in the hugely popular all-Ireland finals on Sunday afternoons in September.  Tickets are available at the stadium except during the finals.

Cost and Hours: €15-55, box office open Mon-Fri 9:30-13:00

DUBLIN

Ireland's Gaelic Athletic Association

The GAA has long been a powerhouse in Ireland. Ireland's national pastimes of Gaelic football and hurling pack stadiums all over the country. When you consider that 80,000 people—paying at least €20 to €30 each—stuff Dublin's Croke Park Stadium and that all the athletes are strictly amateur, you might wonder, "Where does all the money go?"

Ireland has a long tradition of using the revenue generated by these huge events to promote Gaelic athletics and Gaelic cultural events throughout the country in a grassroots and neighborhood way. So, while the players (many of whom are schoolteachers whose jobs allow for evenings and summers free) participate only for the glory of their various counties, the money generated is funding children's leagues, school coaches, small-town athletic facilities, and traditional arts, music, and dance—as well as the building and maintenance of giant stadiums such as Croke Park (which claims to be the third-largest stadium in Europe).

In America, sports are usually considered to be a form of entertainment. But in Ireland, sports have a deeper emotional connection. Gaelic sports are a heartfelt expression of Irish identity. There was a time when the Irish were not allowed to be members of the GAA if they also belonged to a cricket club (a British game).

In 1921, during the War of Independence, Michael Collins (leader of the early IRA, the man who practically invented urban guerrilla warfare) orchestrated the simultaneous assassination of a dozen British intelligence agents around Dublin in a single morning. The same day, the Black and Tans retaliated. These grizzled British WWI veterans, clad in black police coats and tan surplus army pants, had been sent to Ireland to stamp out the rebels. Knowing Croke Park would be full of Irish Nationalists, they entered the packed stadium during a Gaelic football match and fired into the stands, killing 13 spectators as well as a Tipperary player. It was Ireland's first Bloody Sunday, a tragedy that would be repeated 51 years later in Derry.

Today Croke Park's "Hill 16" grandstands are built on rubble dumped here after the 1916 Uprising...literally sacred ground. And the Hogan stands are named after the murdered player from Tipperary. Queen Elizabeth II made it a point to visit the stadium during her historic visit in 2011. Her warm interest in the stadium and in the institution of the GAA did much to heal old wounds.

& 14:15–17:30, tel. 01/871-7400, www.gaa.ie. Choose a county to support, buy something colorful to wear or wave, scream yourself hoarse, and you'll be a temporary local.

Greyhound Racing—For an interesting, lowbrow look at Dublin life, consider going to the dog races and doing a little gambling. Your best bets are Wednesday, Thursday, and Saturday at Shelbourne Park; and Monday, Tuesday, and Friday at Harold's Cross Racetrack.

Cost and Hours: €10, races start at 20:00, tel. 01/497-1081, www.igb.ie.

Shopping in Dublin

Shops are open roughly Monday-Saturday 9:00-18:00 and until 20:00 on Thursday. They have shorter hours on Sunday (if they're open at all). Good shopping areas include:

• **Grafton Street,** with its neighboring streets and arcades (such as the fun Great George's Arcade between Great George's and Drury Streets), and nearby shopping centers (Powerscourt Townhouse and St. Stephen's Green). Francis Street creaks with antiques.

• **Henry Street,** home to Dublin's top department stores (pedestrian-only, off O'Connell Street).

• **Nassau Street,** lining Trinity College, with the popular Kilkenny department store, the Irish Music store, and lots of touristy shops.

• **Temple Bar,** worth a browse any day for its art, jewelry, New Age paraphernalia, books, music (try Claddagh Records), and gift shops. On Saturdays at Temple Bar's Meeting House Square, it's food in the morning (from 9:00) and books in the afternoon (until 18:00).

• **Millennium Walk,** a trendy lane stretching two blocks north from the River Liffey to Abbey Street. It's filled with hip restaurants, shops, and coffee bars. It's easy to miss—look for the south entry at the pedestrian Millennium Bridge, or the north entry at Jervis Street LUAS stop.

• **Street markets,** such as Moore Street (produce, noise, and lots of local color, Mon-Sat 8:00-18:00, closed Sun, near General Post Office), and St. Michan Street (fish, Tue-Sat 7:00-15:00, closed Sun-Mon, behind Four Courts building).

Entertainment in Dublin

Ireland has produced some of the finest writers in both English and Irish, and Dublin houses some of Europe's best theaters. Though the city was the site of the first performance of Handel's *Messiah*

(1742), these days Dublin is famous for its rock bands: U2, Thin Lizzy, Sinéad O'Connor, and Live Aid founder Bob Geldof's band the Boomtown Rats all started here.

Abbey Theatre is Ireland's national theater, founded by W. B. Yeats in 1904 to preserve Irish culture during British rule (€20-40, generally nightly at 19:30, Sat matinees, 26 Lower Abbey Street, tel. 01/878-7222, www.abbeytheatre.ie). **Gate Theatre** does foreign plays as well as Irish classics (Cavendish Row, tel. 01/874-4045, www.gatetheatre.ie). The **Gaiety Theatre** offers a wide range of quality productions (King Street South, tel. 01/677-1717, www.gaietytheatre.com). Street theater takes the stage in Temple Bar on summer evenings. Browse the listings and fliers at the TI.

O2 Theatre, once a railway terminus (easy LUAS access), is now sponsored by a hip phone company. Residents call it by its geographic nickname: The Point. It's considered the country's top live-music venue and is easy to find near the Ferris wheel (East Link Bridge, tel. 01/676-6170 or 01/676-6154, www.theO2.ie).

At the **National Concert Hall,** the National Symphony Orchestra performs most Friday evenings (€20-40, off St. Stephen's Green at Earlsfort Terrace, tel. 01/417-0000, www.nch.ie).

Pub Action: Folk music fills Dublin's pubs, and street entertainers ply their trade in the midst of the party people in Temple Bar and among shoppers on Grafton Street. The Temple Bar area in particular thrives with music—traditional, jazz, and pop. Although it's pricier than the rest of Dublin, it really is the best place for tourists and locals (who come here to watch the tourists).

Gogarty's Pub has top-notch sessions downstairs daily at 14:00 and upstairs nightly from 21:00 (at corner of Fleet and Anglesea, tel. 01/671-1822). Use this pub as a kickoff for your Temple Bar evening. It's also where the Traditional Irish Musical Pub Crawl starts.

A 10-minute hike up the river west of Temple Bar takes you to a twosome with a local and less-touristy ambience. **The Brazen Head,** which lays claim to being the oldest pub in Dublin, is a hit for an early dinner and late live music (nightly from 21:30), with atmospheric rooms and a courtyard perfect for balmy evenings. They also host "Food, Folk, and Fairies" evenings, a great value even at €44. You get a hearty four-course meal punctuated between courses by soulful Irish history and fascinating Irish mythology (April-Nov Tue-Sun 19:00-22:00, Dec-March Wed and Sat; by south end of Father Matthew Bridge, 2 blocks west of Christ Church Cathedral at 20 Bridge Street; pub tel. 01/677-9549, show tel. 01/492-2543, www.irishfolktours.com). **O'Shea's Merchant Pub,** just across the street, is encrusted in memories and filled with locals taking a break from the grind. They have live traditional music nightly at 21:30 (the front half is a restaurant, the magic is in the back half—enter on Bridge Street, tel. 01/679-3797).

At **Palace Bar,** climb upstairs to a cozy room that is a favorite for traditional-music sessions (at east end of Temple Bar, where Fleet Street hits Westmoreland Street at 21 Fleet Street).

Porterhouse has an inviting and varied menu, Dublin's best selection of microbrews, and live music. You won't find Guinness here, just tasty homebrews. Try one of their fun sampler trays. You can check their music schedule online (€12-15 entrées, corner of Essex Street East and Parliament Street, tel. 01/671-5715, www.porterhousebrewco.com/livetemplebar.html).

Pubs at two locations of the **Arlington Hotel** host Irish music and dinner shows. At either place, you'll be entertained by an Irish Rovers-type band singing ballads and a dance troupe scuffing up the floorboards to the delight of tour groups (€30, shows nightly 21:00-23:00, dinner reservations required, www.arlington hoteltemplebar.com). The Arlington Hotel O'Connell Bridge is north of the River Liffey at 23 Bachelors Walk, just off the north end of O'Connell Bridge (tel. 01/804-9100). The Arlington Hotel Temple Bar is south of the river at the corner of Lord Edward Street and Exchange Street Upper, roughly opposite City Hall (tel. 01/670-8777). Make sure you know at which location you're booking reservations.

To sample truly traditional Irish song and dance, consider heading to **Comhaltas Ceoltoiri Éireann** in nearby Dun Laoghaire.

Sleeping in Dublin

Dublin is popular, loud, and expensive. Rooms can be tight. Book ahead for weekends any time of year, particularly in summer and during rugby weekends. In summer, occasional big rock concerts can make rooms hard to find. On Sundays in September, fans converge on Dublin from all over the country for the all-Ireland finals in Gaelic football and hurling. Prices are often discounted on weeknights (Mon-Thu) and from November through February. Check for specials on hotel websites.

Big and practical places (both cheap and moderate) are most central near Christ Church Cathedral, on the edge of Temple Bar.

DUBLIN

Sleep Code

(€1 = about $1.40, country code: 353, area code: 01)
S = Single, **D** = Double/Twin, **T** = Triple, **Q** = Quad, **b** = bathroom,
s = shower only. Breakfast is included and credit cards are
accepted unless otherwise noted.

To help you easily sort through these listings, I've divided
the accommodations into three categories, based on the price
for a standard double room with bath:

  $$$ **Higher Priced**—Most rooms €150 or more.
   $$ **Moderately Priced**—Most rooms between €85-150.
    $ **Lower Priced**—Most rooms €85 or less.

Prices can change without notice; verify the hotel's
current rates online or by email. For other updates, see www
.ricksteves.com/update.

For classy, older Dublin accommodations, you'll stay a bit farther
out (southeast of St. Stephen's Green). If you're a light sleeper or
on a tight budget, get a room in quiet Dun Laoghaire or small-
town Howth, where rooms are roughly one-fourth cheaper. Both
are an easy 25-minute DART train ride into the city.

South of the River Liffey
Near Christ Church Cathedral
These hotels cluster near Christ Church Cathedral, a five-minute
walk from the best evening scene (at Temple Bar), and 10 minutes from the sightseeing center (Trinity College and Grafton
Street). The cheap hostels in this neighborhood have some double rooms. Full Irish breakfasts, which cost €10-12 at the hotels,
are half that price at the many small cafés nearby; try the **Queen
of Tarts** or **Chorus Café** (see listings under "Eating in Dublin,"
later).

$$ Jurys Inn Christ Church, one of three Jurys Inns in down-
town Dublin, is central and offers business-class comfort in all of
its 182 identical rooms. This no-nonsense, American-style hotel
chain has a winning keep-it-simple-and-affordable formula. If ye
olde is getting old—and you don't mind big tour groups—these
are a good option (€79-119 Sun-Thu; €109-149 Fri-Sat for one, two,
or three adults or two adults and two kids; breakfast-€10.50). Its
four floors are strictly non-smoking. Request a room far from the
noisy elevator (book long in advance for weekends, check website
for discounts, pay Wi-Fi in lobby, parking-€15/day, Christ Church
Place, tel. 01/454-0000, fax 01/454-0012, US tel. 800-423-6953,
www.jurysinns.com, jurysinnchristchurch@jurysinns.com). The

other Jurys Inns, described later, are near Connolly Station and Parnell Square.

$$ Harding Hotel is a hardworking, hardwood place with 55 earth-tone rooms that get stuffy on rare hot days (Sb-€55-70; Db-€70-97 Sun-Thu, or €99-120 Fri-Sat; extra bed-€25, breakfast-€7.50; Rick Steves' readers get 10 percent discount in 2012 if booking by email, phone, or fax—but not online; on weekends, request a quiet upper-floor room away from the fun but noisy ground-floor pub; free Wi-Fi, on Fishamble Street across the street from Christ Church Cathedral, tel. 01/679-6500, fax 01/679-6504, www.hardinghotel.ie, info@hardinghotel.ie).

$ Kinlay House, around the corner from Harding Hotel, is the backpackers' choice—definitely the place to go for cheap beds, a central location, and an all-ages-welcome atmosphere. This huge, red-brick, 19th-century Victorian building has 200 metal, prison-style beds in spartan, non-smoking rooms. There are singles, doubles, and four- to six-bed coed dorms (good for families), as well as a few giant dorms. It fills up most days—call well in advance, especially for singles, doubles, and summer weekends (S-€40-50, Sb-€45-60, D-€50-60, Db-€60-66, T-€72-87, Tb-€87-96, dorm beds-€20-26, includes continental breakfast, free Internet access and Wi-Fi, free 10-minute international phone call, kitchen access, launderette-€8, left luggage-€1/day, travel desk, TV lounge, small lockers-€1/day, lots of stairs, Christ Church, 2-12 Lord Edward Street, tel. 01/679-6644, fax 01/679-7437, www.kinlaydublin.ie, info@kinlaydublin.ie).

$ Four Courts Hostel is a 234-bed hostel beautifully located immediately across the river from the Four Courts. It's within a five-minute walk of Christ Church Cathedral and Temple Bar. Bare and institutional (as hostels typically are), it's also spacious and well-run, with a focus on security and efficiency (dorm beds-€15-24, S-€35, Sb-€38-45, bunk D-€40, bunk Db-€45-50, includes small breakfast, non-smoking, elevator, free Internet access and Wi-Fi, free 10-minute international phone call, game room, laundry service, some parking-€10/day, left-luggage room; 15-17 Merchant's Quay, bus #90 from Connolly Station or Busáras Central Bus Station; tel. 01/672-5839, www.fourcourtshostel.com, info@fourcourtshostel.com).

Trinity College Area

You can't get more central than Trinity College; these two listings offer a good value for what you're spending.

$$$ Trinity Lodge offers fine quiet lodging in 24 rooms split between two Georgian townhouses on either side of Frederick Street South, just south of Trinity College (Sb-€90-140, Db-€89-165, Tb-€149-219, Qb-€159-249, Wi-Fi, 12 South Frederick Street,

DUBLIN

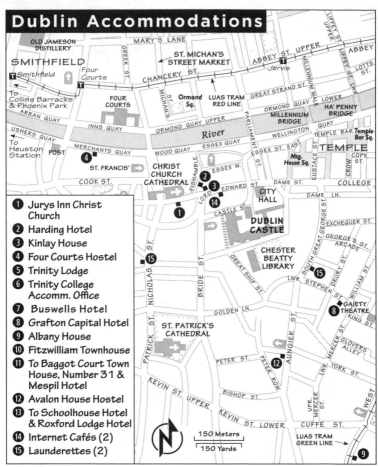

Dublin Accommodations

1. Jurys Inn Christ Church
2. Harding Hotel
3. Kinlay House
4. Four Courts Hostel
5. Trinity Lodge
6. Trinity College Accomm. Office
7. Buswells Hotel
8. Grafton Capital Hotel
9. Albany House
10. Fitzwilliam Townhouse
11. To Baggot Court Town House, Number 31 & Mespil Hotel
12. Avalon House Hostel
13. To Schoolhouse Hotel & Roxford Lodge Hotel
14. Internet Cafés (2)
15. Launderettes (2)

tel. 01/617-0900, fax 01/617-0999, www.trinitylodge.com, trinity lodge@eircom.net).

$$ Trinity College turns its 800 student-housing rooms on campus into no-frills, affordable accommodations in the city center each summer. Look for the easy-to-miss Accommodations Office (open Mon-Fri 9:00-12:45 & 14:00-17:00) inside the huge courtyard, 50 yards down the wall on the left from the main entry arch (late-May-mid-Sept, S-€60.50, Sb-€74.50, D-€81, Db-€125, includes continental breakfast, cooked breakfast-€4 extra, tel. 01/896-1177, fax 01/671-1267, www.tcd.ie/accommodation/visitors, reservations@tcd.ie).

Near St. Stephen's Green

Dublin is filled with worn-yet-comfy townhouses. Albany House,

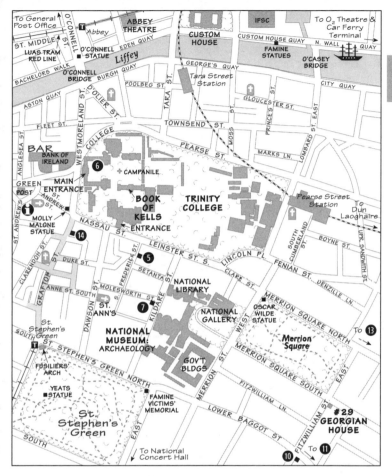

Fitzwilliam Townhouse, and Baggot Court Town House are dependable, basic lodgings, while the first two hotels are cushier.

$$ Buswells Hotel, one of the city's oldest, is a pleasant Georgian-style haven with 67 reasonably priced rooms in the heart of the city (Sb-€109-129, Db-€129-149, Tb-€149-169, free Wi-Fi, between Trinity College and St. Stephen's Green at 23-25 Molesworth Street, tel. 01/614-6500, fax 01/676-2090, www.buswells.ie, enquiries@buswells.ie).

$$ Grafton Capital Hotel has a good central location and fine rooms. The popular downstairs pub is noisy on weekend nights, so light sleepers should request a room facing the back (Db-€59-139, Tb-€99-169, breakfast-€10, three non-smoking floors, Wi-Fi in lobby, 2 blocks west of St. Stephen's Green on Lower Stephen's Street, tel. 01/648-1100, fax 01/648-1122, www.capital-hotels.com, info@graftoncapital-hotel.com).

$$ Albany House's 43 restful rooms come with high ceilings, Georgian elegance, and some street noise—request a quieter room at the back (Sb-€60-110, Db-€120-140, Tb-€120-170, Una promises 10 percent off when booking direct by phone or email with this book in 2012, non-smoking, Wi-Fi in lobby, just one block south of St. Stephen's Green at 84 Harcourt Street, tel. 01/475-1092, fax 01/475-1093, www.albanyhousedublin.com, albany@indigo.ie).

$$ Fitzwilliam Townhouse rents 14 good-value rooms in a Georgian townhouse near St. Stephen's Green (Sb-€49-85, Db-€59-109, Tb-€75-119, Qb-€85-129, breakfast-€6.50-9.50, all rooms non-smoking, free Wi-Fi, 41 Upper Fitzwilliam Street, tel. 01/662-5155, fax 01/676-7488, www.fitzwilliamtownhouse.com, info@fitzwilliamtownhouse.com).

$$ Baggot Court Town House, with the same owners as the Fitzwilliam (above), has 16 nice rooms a block farther on from St. Stephen's Green (Sb-€55-105, Db-€65-139, Tb-€89-149, non-smoking, free Wi-Fi, free parking, 92 Lower Baggot Street, tel. 01/661-2819, fax 01/661-0253, www.baggotcourt.com, reservations @baggotcourt.com).

$ Avalon House Hostel, near Grafton Street, rents 282 simple, clean backpacker beds in refurbished rooms (dorm beds-€14-26, S-€25-30, Sb-€37-41, twin D-€50-68, twin Db-€60-78, includes continental breakfast, elevator, free Internet access and Wi-Fi, launderette, kitchen, lockers-€1/day, helpful staff, a few minutes off Grafton Street at 55 Aungier Street, tel. 01/475-0001, fax 01/475-0303, www.avalon-house.ie, info@avalon-house.ie).

Away from the Center, Southeast of St. Stephen's Green

The listings that follow are unique places (except for the business-class Mespil Hotel), and charge accordingly. If you're going to break the bank, do it here.

$$$ Number 31 is a hidden gem reached via gritty little Leeson Close (a lane off Lower Leeson Street). Its understated elegance is top-notch, with 6 rooms in a former coach house and 15 rooms in an adjacent Georgian house; the two buildings are connected by a quiet little garden. Guests appreciate the special touches (such as a sunken living room) and tasty breakfasts served in a classy glass atrium (Sb-€100-140, Db-€180-220, Tb-€240-280, Qb-€280-340, all non-smoking, Wi-Fi, free parking, 31 Leeson Close, tel. 01/676-5011, fax 01/676-2929, www.number31 .ie, info@number31.ie).

$$$ The Schoolhouse Hotel taught as many as 300 students in its heyday (1861-1969) and was in the middle of the street fight of the 1916 Easter Uprising. Now it's a serene hideout with 31 pristine rooms and a fine restaurant (Sb-€89-169, Db-€99-179, book early, Wi-Fi, 2-8 Northumberland Road, tel. 01/667-5014, fax 01/667-5015, www.schoolhousehotel.com, info@schoolhouse hotel.com).

DUBLIN

$$$ Mespil Hotel is a huge, modern, business-class hotel renting 255 identical three-star rooms (most with a double and single bed, phone, TV, and voicemail) at a good price with all the comforts. This place is a cut above Jurys Inn (Sb, Db, or Tb-€79-195, breakfast-€10, elevator, non-smoking floors, free Wi-Fi; small first-come, first-served free parking; apartments for weeklong stays; 10-minute walk southeast of St. Stephen's Green or take bus #37, #38, or #39, 50-60 Mespil Road; tel. 01/488-4600, fax 01/667-1244, www.mespilhotel.com, mespil@leehotels.com).

$$ Roxford Lodge Hotel is a memorable splurge. In a quiet residential neighborhood a 20-minute walk from Trinity College, it has 20 tastefully decorated rooms awash with Jacuzzis and saunas. The €150-200 executive suite is honeymoon-worthy (Sb-€69-99, Db-€89-140, Tb-€85-150, Qb-€95-170, breakfast-€12, free Wi-Fi, secure free parking, 46 Northumberland Road, tel. 01/668-8572, fax 01/668-8158, www.roxfordlodge.ie, reservations @roxfordlodge.ie).

North of the River Liffey
Near Connolly Station
This once-tattered neighborhood (like much of the north side) is gradually becoming rejuvenated..

$$ Jurys Inn Custom House, on Custom House Quay, offers the same value as the other Jurys Inns in Dublin, but it's less central. Its 239 rooms border the financial district, a 10-minute riverside hike from O'Connell Bridge. Of the three Jurys Inns in town, this one is most likely to have rooms available (Db-€79-119 Sun-Thu, or €109-149 Fri-Sat, breakfast-€10.50, pay Wi-Fi, parking-€15/day, tel. 01/854-1500, fax 01/829-0400, US tel. 800-423-6953, www.jurysinns.com, jurysinncustomhouse@jurysinns.com).

$$ The Townhouse, with 81 small, stylish rooms (some with pleasant views into a central garden courtyard), hides behind a brick Georgian facade one block north of the Customs House (Sb-€49-70, Db-€60-120, Tb-€75-144, Internet access and Wi-Fi; small first-come, first-served parking lot; 47-48 Lower Gardiner Street, tel. 01/878-8808, fax 01/878-8787, www.townhouseofdublin .com, info@townhouseofdublin.com).

Near Parnell Square
A swanky neighborhood 200 years ago, this is now workaday Dublin with a steady urban hum.

$$ Jurys Inn Parnell Street, built in 2006 as part of the steady gentrification of Dublin's north side, has 253 predictably soulless but good-value rooms. It's a block from the north end of O'Connell Street and the cluster of museums on Parnell Square (Db-€79-119 Sun-Thu, or €129-149 Fri-Sat, breakfast-€10.50, pay Wi-Fi in lobby, tel. 01/878-4900, fax 01/878-4999, www.jurysinns .com, jurysinnparnellst@jurysinns.com).

$$ Belvedere Hotel has 92 plain-vanilla rooms that are short on character but long on dependable, modern comforts (Db-€69-99 Sun-Thu, or €89-129 Fri-Sat, cheaper if booked online, free Wi-Fi in some rooms, Great Denmark Street, tel. 01/873-7700, fax 01/873-7776, www.belvederehotel.ie, reservations@belvedere hotel.ie).

$ Charles Stewart Guesthouse, big and basic, offers 60 forgettable rooms. But it's in a great location for a good price (Sb-€45-59, Db-€50-79, Tb-€75-119, Qb-€89-139, frequent midweek discounts, includes cooked breakfast, ask for a quieter room in the back, free Wi-Fi, just beyond top end of O'Connell Street at 5-6 Parnell Square East, tel. 01/878-0350, fax 01/878-1387, www.charles stewart.ie, sales@charlesstewart.ie).

Eating in Dublin

It's easy to find fine, creative eateries all over town. While you can get decent pub grub for €12-15 on just about any corner, consider saving that for the countryside. There's just no pressing reason to eat Irish in cosmopolitan Dublin. In fact, going local these days is the same as going ethnic. The city's good restaurants are packed from 20:00 on, especially on weekends. Eating early (17:30-19:00) saves time and money, as many better places offer an early-bird special. Many restaurants serve free jugs of ice water with a smile.

Quick and Easy near Grafton Street

Cornucopia is a small, earth-mama-with-class, proudly vegetarian, self-serve place two blocks off Grafton. It's friendly and youthful, with hearty €12 lunches and €15 dinner specials (Mon-Wed 8:30-21:00, Thu-Sat 8:30-22:30, Sun 12:00-20:30, 19 Wicklow Street, tel. 01/677-7583).

The Farm, Dublin's healthiest dining option, shuns processed food and features fresh, organic, and free-range fare that's affordable and pretty darn tasty (€15-25 main courses, €20 two-course and €24 three-course early-bird specials, daily 11:00-23:00, a half-block south of Trinity College at 3 Dawson Street, tel. 01/671-8654).

O'Neill's Pub is a venerable, dark, and tangled retreat offering good grub, including dependable €11-15 carvery lunches. It's very central, located across from the main TI (daily 12:00-22:00, Suffolk Street, tel. 01/679-3656).

Two pubs on Duke Street—**The Duke** and **Davy Burns**—serve reliable pub lunches. (The nearby Cathach Rare Books shop, at 10 Duke Street, displays a rare edition of *Ulysses* inscribed by Joyce, among other treasures, in its window.)

Bewley's Café is an old-time favorite, offering light meals from €10 and full meals from €12-17. Sit on the ground floor among Art Deco lamps and windows by stained-glass artist Harry Clarke, or head upstairs to the bright atrium decorated by art students (self-service Mon-Sat 8:00-22:00, Sun 9:00-22:00, 78 Grafton Street, tel. 01/672-7720). For a taste of witty Irish lunch theater, check out **Bewley's Café Theatre** upstairs; you can catch a fun hour-long performance while having a lunch of soup and brown bread for €15 (Mon-Sat at 13:00 during a play's run—doors open at 12:45, closed Sun, booking info mobile 086-878-4001, www.bewleyscafe theatre.com).

Wagamama Noodle Bar, like its popular sisters in Britain, is a pan-Asian slurp-a-thon with great and healthy noodle and rice dishes (€12-17) served at long communal tables by energetic waiters (daily 12:00-23:00, no reservations, often a line but it moves quickly, South King Street underneath St. Stephen's Green Shopping Centre, tel. 01/478-2152).

South Great George's Street is lined with hardworking little eateries. **Juice** keeps vegetarians happy (daily 12:00-22:00, 73 South Great George's Street, tel. 01/475-7856).

Yamamori is a plain, mellow, and modern Japanese place serving seas of sushi and noodles (€10-15 lunches daily 12:00-17:30, €16-20 dinners nightly 17:30-23:00, 71 South Great George's Street, tel. 01/475-5001).

Supermarkets: **Dunnes,** on South Great George's Street, is your one-stop shop for assembling a picnic meal (Mon-Sat 8:30-19:00, Sun 11:00-19:00, across from Yamamori). They have another outlet in the basement of the St. Stephen's Green Shopping Centre. **Marks & Spencer** department store has a fancy grocery store in the basement, with fine take-away sandwiches and salads (Mon-Fri 9:00-20:00, Thu until 21:00, Sat 8:30-20:00, Sun 11:00-19:00, Grafton Street).

Hip and Fun in North Dublin

The Church is a trendy café/bar/restaurant/nightclub/beer garden housed in the former St. Mary's Church. In its former life as a church, it hosted the baptism of Irish rebel Wolfe Tone and the marriage of brewing legend Arthur Guinness. The choir balcony has a huge pipe organ and a refined menu; the ground floor nave is dominated by a long bar and pub grub; and a disco thumps like

DUBLIN

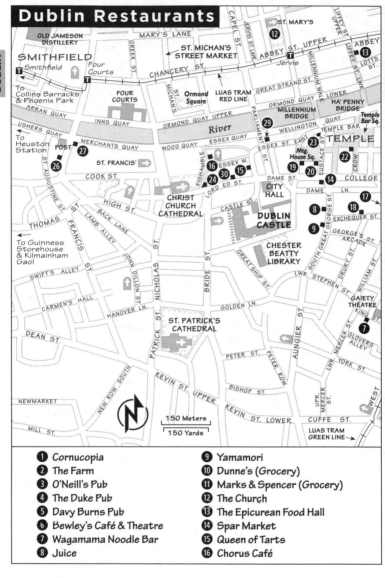

Dublin Restaurants

1 Cornucopia
2 The Farm
3 O'Neill's Pub
4 The Duke Pub
5 Davy Burns Pub
6 Bewley's Café & Theatre
7 Wagamama Noodle Bar
8 Juice
9 Yamamori
10 Dunne's (Grocery)
11 Marks & Spencer (Grocery)
12 The Church
13 The Epicurean Food Hall
14 Spar Market
15 Queen of Tarts
16 Chorus Café

hell in the bunker-like basement. On warm summer nights, the outdoor terrace is packed. Eating here is as much about the scene as the cuisine (pub grub daily 12:00-20:00, balcony restaurant open daily 17:00-22:30, €25 four-course early-bird special before 19:00, reservations smart Fri and Sat nights, corner of St. Mary's and Jervis Streets, tel. 01/828-0102).

The Epicurean Food Hall offers a fun selection of food stalls

DUBLIN

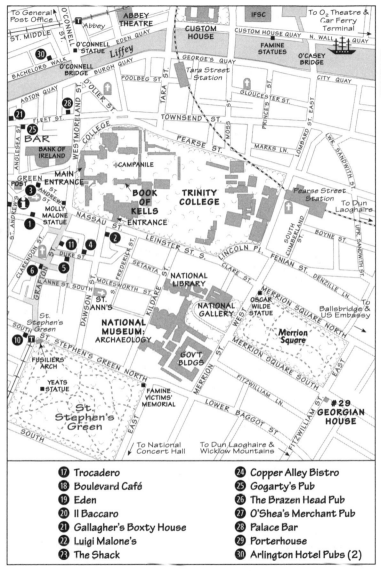

⑰ Trocadero	㉔ Copper Alley Bistro
⑱ Boulevard Café	㉕ Gogarty's Pub
⑲ Eden	㉖ The Brazen Head Pub
⑳ Il Baccaro	㉗ O'Shea's Merchant Pub
㉑ Gallagher's Boxty House	㉘ Palace Bar
㉒ Luigi Malone's	㉙ Porterhouse
㉓ The Shack	㉚ Arlington Hotel Pubs (2)

with big and splittable portions. It's a hit with locals—and visitors—needing to eat cheaply (100 yards north of the Ha' Penny Bridge on Lower Liffey Street).

Fast and Cheap near Christ Church Cathedral

Many of Dublin's late-night grocery stores sell cheap salads, microwaved meat pies, and made-to-order sandwiches (such as

Spar Market, open 24 hours a day, off the top of Dame Street on Parliament Street). A €10 picnic dinner brought back to the hotel might be a good option after a busy day of sightseeing.

Queen of Tarts does yummy breakfasts, fruit salads, sandwiches, and wonderful pastries with quiet streetside seating. Get yours to go, and enjoy a picnic with a Georgian view in one of Dublin's grassy squares (€6-8 breakfasts, €8-12 lunches, Mon-Fri 8:00-19:00, Sat-Sun 9:00-19:00, hidden beside Kinlay House on Cow's Lane, tel. 01/670-7499).

Chorus Café is a friendly little hole-in-the-wall diner, perfect for breakfast, lunch, or dinner with a newspaper (€8 breakfasts, €10 lunches, €12-18 dinners, Mon-Fri 8:30-22:00, Sat 9:30-22:00, closed Sun, Fishamble Street, next door to the site of the first performance of Handel's *Messiah*, tel. 01/616-7088).

Dining at Classy Restaurants and Cafés

These two stylish restaurants serve well-presented food at fair prices. They're located within a block of each other, just south of Temple Bar and Dame Street, near the main TI.

Trocadero serves beefy European cuisine to Dubliners interested in a slow, romantic meal. The dressy, red-velvet interior is draped with photos of local actors. Come early or make a reservation—it's a favorite with theatergoers (€21-30 meals, Mon-Sat 17:00-24:00, closed Sun, 4 St. Andrew Street, tel. 01/677-5545). The three-course pre-theater special is a fine value at €25 (17:00-19:00, leave by 19:45).

Boulevard Café is mod, trendy, and likeable, dishing up Mediterranean cuisine that's heavy on the Italian. Their salads, pasta, and sandwiches cost roughly €9-15, and three-course lunch specials are €16 (Mon-Sat 10:00-18:00). It's smart to reserve for dinner, which runs about €17-24 (Mon-Sat 12:00-24:00, closed Sun, 27 Exchequer Street, tel. 01/679-2131).

In Temple Bar

Eden is a classy refuge serving a variety of contemporary Irish dishes in an airy space with a pleasant outdoor terrace (€18-27 dishes, Mon-Sat 12:30-15:00 & 17:00-22:00, Sun 12:00-16:00 & 18:00-21:30; on Meeting House Square, a half-block off the busy tourist thoroughfare; tel. 01/670-5372). They offer a three-course pre-theater menu for €27 (Sun-Thu only before 19:00).

Il Baccaro, a cozy Italian wine tavern with an arched brick ceiling, is tucked in a quiet corner of Meeting House Square (€13-18 pasta dinners, daily 17:30-22:30, lunches Sat 12:00-16:00 only, closed Sun, tel. 01/671-4597).

Gallagher's Boxty House is touristy and traditional—a good, basic value with creaky floorboards and old Dublin ambience. Its specialty is the boxty, the generally bland-tasting Irish potato pancake filled and rolled with various meats, veggies, and sauces. The "Gaelic Boxty" is the liveliest (€15-23, daily 11:00-22:30, also serves stews and corned beef, 20 Temple Bar, reservations wise, tel. 01/677-2762).

Luigi Malone's, with its fun atmosphere and varied menu of pizza, ribs, pasta, sandwiches, and fajitas, is just the place to take your high-school date (€13-21 dishes, Mon-Sat 12:00-22:00, Sun 13:00-21:30, corner of Cecilia and Fownes streets, tel. 01/679-2723).

The Shack, while a bit touristy, has a reputation for good quality. It serves traditional Irish, chicken, seafood, and steak dishes (€16-25 entrées, €19 three-course early-bird special offered 17:00-19:00, open daily 12:00-22:00, in the center of Temple Bar, 24 East Essex Street, tel. 01/679-0043).

Copper Alley Bistro, a bit farther from the Temple Bar chaos and more reasonably priced, serves comfort-food lunches and dinners (daily 12:00-21:00, corner of Fishamble and Lord Edward streets, just opposite Christ Church Cathedral, tel. 01/679-6500).

Dublin Connections

Note that trains and buses generally run less frequently on Sundays.

By Train from Dublin's Heuston Station to: Tralee (every two hours, 5/day on Sun, most change in Mallow but one direct evening train, 4 hours), **Ennis** (11/day, 3-3.5 hours), **Galway** (6/day, 2.5-3 hours). Train info: recorded timetable tel. 01/805-4222, www.irishrail.ie.

By Train from Dublin's Connolly Station to: Rosslare (3-4/day, 3 hours), **Portrush** (7/day, 2/day Sun, 5 hours, transfer in Belfast or Coleraine). The **Dublin-Belfast train** connects the two Irish capitals in two hours at 90 mph on one continuous, welded rail (8/day Mon-Sat, 5/day Sun, €36 "day return" tickets, check online for special deals, can cost more Fri-Sun, tel. 01/836-3333). Train info: tel. 01/836-6222. Northern Ireland train info: tel. 048/9089-9400.

By Bus to: Belfast (hourly, most via Dublin Airport, 2.75-3 hours), **Trim** (almost hourly, 1 hour), **Ennis** (almost hourly, 5-5.25 hours), **Galway** (hourly, 3.25 hours; faster on CityLink; hourly, 2.5 hours, tel. 890-280-808, www.citylink.ie), **Limerick** (hourly, 3.75 hours), **Tralee** (8/day, 6 hours), **Dingle** (4/day, 8-9 hours, transfer at Limerick and Tralee). Bus info: tel. 01/836-6111, www.buseireann.ie.

Dublin Airport: The airport is well-connected to the city center seven miles away. Airport info: tel. 01/814-1111, www.dublin airport.ie. Airlines are listed below and in the appendix. To sleep at Dublin Airport, a safe bet is the **$$ Radisson SAS Hotel** (Db-€75-109, best prices if booked online, tel. 01/844-6000, http://hotels.radissonsas.com).

Connecting Ireland and Britain

Spend a few minutes online researching your transportation options across the Irish Sea. Most airline and ferry companies routinely offer discounts (often as much as €10) for tickets purchased from their websites. Before sorting out rail/ferry prices with individual companies, try www.arrivatrainswales.co.uk/sailrail, which deals with several companies and has fares low enough to compete with cheap airlines.

If you're going directly to London, flying is your best bet. Check **Ryanair** first (1.5 hours, Irish tel. 081-830-3030, www .ryanair.com). Other options include **British Airways** (Irish tel. 1-890-626-747, US tel. 800-247-9297, www.ba.com), **Aer Lingus** (tel. 081-836-5000, www.aerlingus.com), and **bmi** (Irish tel. 01/407-3036, US tel. 800-788-0555, www.flybmi.com). To get the lowest fares, ask about round-trip ticket prices and book months in advance (though Ryanair offers deals nearly all the time).

Dublin and Liverpool: P&O has ferries for cars only (2-3/ day, 8.5 hours, tel. 08716-642-020, www.poferries.com). Check in one to two hours before the sailing time—call to confirm details.

Dublin and Holyhead: Irish Ferries sails between Dublin and Holyhead in North Wales. The dock is a mile east of O'Connell Bridge (4/day: 2 slow, 2 fast; slow boats—3.5 hours, €30 one-way walk-on fare; fast boats—2 hours, €35; Dublin tel. 0818-300-400, Holyhead tel. 08705-329-129, www.irishferries.com).

Dun Laoghaire and Holyhead: Stena Line sails a huge catamaran between Dun Laoghaire (near Dublin) and Holyhead in North Wales (1-2/day, 2 hours, only runs in summer, €30 one-way

walk-on fare, €4 extra if paying with credit card, reserve by phone—they book up long in advance on summer weekends, Dun Laoghaire tel. 01/204-7777, recorded info tel. 01/204-7799, can book online at www.stena line.com).

Ferries to France

With the glut of discount airlines that have sprung up over the past decade, it makes little sense to waste your valuable time on a 20-hour-plus ferry ride when you could fly to France in less than 3 hours. Aer Arann connects far-flung western Irish towns to the continent via Dublin or London (www.aerarann.com).

But if the nostalgia of a long, slow ferry ride and the risk of rough seas appeal to you, look into **Irish Ferries,** which connects Ireland (Rosslare) with France (Cherbourg and Roscoff) every other day (less frequently Jan-March). While Cherbourg has the quickest connection to Paris, your overall time between Ireland and Paris is about the same (20-25 hours) regardless of which port is used on the day you sail. One-way fares range from €59 to €69 and are cheapest if booked online. Eurailpass-holders get 30 percent off. In both directions, departures are generally between 15:30 and 16:00 and arrive late the next morning.

While passengers can nearly always get on, reservations are wise in summer and easy by phone. If you anticipate a crowded departure, you can reserve a seat for €15. Cabins (2 beds) go for €69-99. The easiest way to get a bed (except during summer) is from the information desk upon boarding. The cafeteria serves bad food at reasonable prices. Upon arrival in France, buses and taxis connect you to your Paris-bound train (Irish Ferries: Dublin tel. 0818-300-400, www.irishferries.com, info@irishferries.com).

Dun Laoghaire and Howth

Dun Laoghaire (dun LEERY) and Howth (rhymes with "growth") are two peas in a pod, dangling from opposite ends of Dublin Bay's crescent-shaped shoreline. They offer quieter, cheaper lodging alternatives to Dublin. Both offer easy DART light rail access to the city center, just a 25-minute ride away. Each houses its only worthwhile sightseeing options in pillbox martello (masonry) towers. And they were each once home to famous Irish writers: James Joyce in Dun Laoghaire and W. B. Yeats in Howth. The fundamental difference between the two is that Dun Laoghaire (south of Dublin) has the ferry port to Wales, while Howth (north of Dublin) is closer to the airport.

Dun Laoghaire

Dun Laoghaire is seven miles south of Dublin. This snoozy suburb, with the ferry terminal for Wales and easy connections to downtown Dublin, is a great small-town base for exploring the

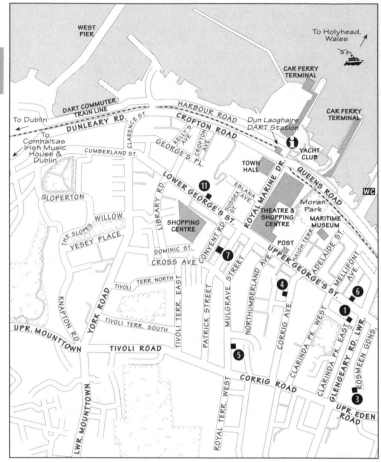

big city.

The Dun Laoghaire harbor was strategic enough to merit a line of martello towers, built to defend against an expected Napoleonic invasion (one tower now houses the James Joyce Museum). By the mid-19th century, its

massive breakwaters were completed, protecting a huge harbor. Ships sailed regularly from here to Wales (75 miles away), and the first train line in Ireland connected the terminal with Dublin.

DUBLIN

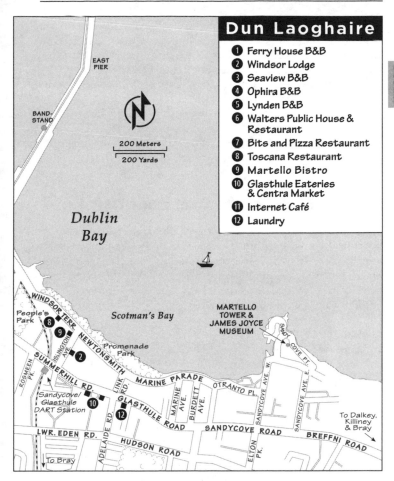

Dun Laoghaire

1. Ferry House B&B
2. Windsor Lodge
3. Seaview B&B
4. Ophira B&B
5. Lynden B&B
6. Walters Public House & Restaurant
7. Bits and Pizza Restaurant
8. Toscana Restaurant
9. Martello Bistro
10. Glasthule Eateries & Centra Market
11. Internet Café
12. Laundry

Getting to Dun Laoghaire

Buses run between Dublin and Dun Laoghaire, but the **DART** commuter train is much faster and not subject to Dublin traffic delays (4/hour, 25 minutes, runs Mon-Sat about 6:00-23:30, Sun from 9:00, €2.40 one-way, €4.40 round-trips are good same day only, 3-day pass-€11.80, Eurailpass valid but uses a flexi-day, tel. 01/703-3504, www.irishrail.ie). If you're coming from Dublin, catch a DART train marked "Bray" and get off at the Sandycove/ Glasthule or Dun Laoghaire stop, depending on which B&B you choose. If you're leaving Dun Laoghaire, catch a train marked "Howth" to get to Dublin. Get off at the central Tara Street Station if you want to sightsee in Dublin; or, for train connections north (or the Airlink bus to the airport), ride it one stop farther to Connolly Station.

The **Aircoach bus** goes to and from the Dublin Airport via the Port Tunnel. You can catch it at either the Town Hall in Dun Laoghaire or opposite St. Joseph's Church in nearby Glasthule (€8, departs Dun Laoghaire starting at 4:00 and from the airport's short-term parking lot starting at 5:00 until 23:00, hourly, 50 minutes, tel. 01/844-7118, www.aircoach.ie).

The **taxi** fare from Dun Laoghaire to central Dublin is about €35; to the airport, about €50. Try ABC Taxi service (tel. 01/285-5444). With DART access into Dublin, and cheap or sometimes free parking, Dun Laoghaire is ideal for those with **cars** (which can cost more than €30/day to park in Dublin).

Orientation to Dun Laoghaire

A busy transportation hub, Dun Laoghaire has a coastline defined by its nearly mile-long breakwaters—reaching like two muscular arms into the Irish Sea. The breakwaters are popular for strollers, bikers, bird-watchers, and fishermen.

Tourist Information: The TI is in the ferry terminal (Mon-Sat 10:00-12:45 & 14:00-18:00, closed Sun).

Helpful Hints

Internet Access: Central Internet Café provides a fast connection (€4/hour, Mon-Fri 9:00-22:00, Sat 10:00-20:00, Sun 11:00-22:00, 88B Lower George's Street, tel. 01/231-1186).

Post Office: It's on Lower George's Street (Mon-Fri 9:00-18:00, Sat 9:00-13:00, closed Sun).

Laundry: Try **Jeeves,** located in the village of Glasthule, a five-minute downhill walk from Sandycove/Glasthule DART station (Mon-Fri 8:30-18:00, Sat 9:00-18:00, closed Sun, full-service only, 34 Glasthule Road, next to Daniel's Restaurant and Wine Bar, tel. 01/230-1120).

Parking: If you don't have free parking at your B&B, try the pay-and-display street-parking system. Buy a ticket at machines spaced along the street, and display it on your dashboard (Mon-Fri 8:00-19:00, €1/hour, 3-hour max, free Sat-Sun).

Best Views: Hike out to the lighthouse, at the end of the interesting East Pier; or climb the tight stairs to the top of the James Joyce Museum/tower.

Sights in Dun Laoghaire

James Joyce Museum—This squat martello tower at Sandycove was originally built to repel a Napoleonic invasion, but it became famous chiefly because of its association with James Joyce. The great author lived here briefly and made it the setting for the opening of his novel *Ulysses*. Today, the museum's round exhibition space is filled with literary memorabilia, including photographs and rare first editions. For a fine view, climb the claustrophobic, two-story spiral stairwell sealed inside the thick wall to reach the rooftop gun mount.

Cost and Hours: €6, €11.50 combo-ticket with Dublin Writers' Museum, March-Oct Tue-Sat 10:00-13:00 & 14:00-17:00, Sun 14:00-18:00, closed Mon, open by appointment only Nov-Feb, tel. 01/280-9265.

Swimming—Kids of all ages enjoy swimming at the safe, sandy little cove bordered by rounded rocks beside the martello tower.

Entertainment in Dun Laoghaire

For an evening of pure Irish music, song, and dance, check out the **Comhaltas Ceoltoiri Éireann,** an association working to preserve this slice of Irish culture. It got started in the 1950s when Elvis and company threatened to steal the musical heart of the new generation. Judging by the pop status of traditional Irish music these days, Comhaltas has accomplished its mission. Their Seisiun evening is a stage show mixing traditional music, song, and dance (€10, July-Aug Mon-Thu at 21:00, followed by informal music session at 22:30). On Fridays all year long, they have a *ceilidh* (KAY-lee), where everyone does set dances. This style, the forerunner of square dancing, evolved from the French Quadrille dances of 200 years ago, with two couples making up a set (€10 includes friendly pointers, 21:30-24:30). At 21:00 on Tuesdays and Wednesdays (free) and Saturdays (€3), there are informal sessions by the fireside. All musicians are welcome. Performances are held at the Cuturlann na Éireann center at 32 Belgrave Square in Monkstown (near the Seapoint DART stop, or take bus #7 from Dun Laoghaire, tel. 01/280-0295, www.comhaltas.ie). Their bar is free to enter (no cover charge) and often filled with music.

Sleeping in Dun Laoghaire

(€1 = about $1.40, country code: 353, area code: 01)

In Dun Laoghaire, near Sandycove DART Station

These listings are within a couple of blocks of the Sandycove/Glasthule DART station and a 10-minute walk to the Dun Laoghaire DART station/ferry landing.

$ Ferry House B&B, with four high-ceilinged rooms, is a family-friendly place on a dead-end street (Sb-€45-60, Db-€65-75, Tb-€90-100, Qb-€110, €5 discount with cash and direct booking, non-smoking, Wi-Fi, 15 Clarinda Park North just off Clarinda Park West, tel. 01/280-8301, www.ferryhousedublin.com, ferry_house@hotmail.com, Eamon and Pauline Teehan).

$ Windsor Lodge rents four fresh, inviting rooms on a quiet street a block off the harbor and a block from the DART station (Db-€50-70, Tb-€90, cash only, non-smoking, Wi-Fi, 3 Islington Avenue, tel. 01/284-6952, mobile 086-844-6646, www.windsor lodge.ie, windsorlodgedublin@gmail.com, Mary O'Farrell).

$ Seaview B&B, a modern house run by Mrs. Kane, has three big, cheery rooms and a welcoming guests' lounge with a bright and friendly feeling (S-€35, Db-€70 with this book in 2012, cash only, non-smoking, just above Rosmeen Gardens at 2 Granite Hall, tel. & fax 01/280-9105, www.seaviewbedandbreakfast.com, seaviewbedandbreakfast@hotmail.com).

Near the Dun Laoghaire DART Station

$ Ophira B&B is a historic house with four comfortably creaky rooms run by active diver, hiker, and biker John O'Connor (Sb-€40-55, Db-€55-75, Tb-€75-100, Qb-€100-140, non-smoking, Wi-Fi, parking available, 10 Corrig Avenue, tel. 01/280-0997, www.ophira.ie, info@ophira.ie).

$ Lynden B&B, with a classy 150-year-old interior hiding behind a somber front, rents four big rooms (S-€35-40, D-€55-60, Db-€65-70, Wi-Fi, go past Mulgrave Street to 2 Mulgrave Terrace, tel. 01/280-6404, fax 01/230-2258, www.lyndenbandb .com, lynden@iol.ie, Maria Gavin).

Eating in Dun Laoghaire

If staying in Dun Laoghaire, I'd definitely eat here rather than in Dublin.

George's Street, Dun Laoghaire's main drag three blocks inland, has plenty of eateries and pubs, many with live music. **Walters Public House and Restaurant** is a bright, modern place above a pub, offering good food to a dressy crowd. The multi-terraced back patio of the pub is great for a drink on a warm evening (€16-26 meals, €8-14 pub meals, daily 17:30-22:00, 68 Upper George's Street, tel. 01/280-7442). A good bet for families is the kid-friendly **Bits and Pizza** (daily 12:00-22:00, off George's Street at 15 Patrick Street, tel. 01/284-2411).

Toscana, on the seafront, is a popular little cubbyhole, serving hearty Italian dishes and pizza. Its prime location makes it easy to incorporate into your evening stroll. Reserve for dinner (€11-24 meals, daily 12:00-22:00, 5 Windsor Terrace, tel. 01/230-0890).

Martello Bistro, also on the stroll-worthy waterfront, is a good bet for seafood or steak in a friendly atmosphere (daily 17:00-

22:30, €23 for two courses, €26 for three courses, 1 Martello Terrace, tel. 01/280-9871).

Glasthule (called simply "the village" locally, just down the street from the Sandycove/Glasthule DART station) has an array of fun, hardworking little restaurants. The big **Eagle House pub** dishes up great Indian food and hearty €10-19 pub meals in a wonderful atmosphere; it's a super local joint for a late drink (Mon-Sat 12:30-21:30, Sun 12:30-19:30, 18-19 Glasthule Road, tel. 01/280-4740). The nearby **Daniel's Restaurant and Wine Bar** is less atmospheric, but it's also good (€18-24 meals, Tue-Sun 18:00-22:30, closed Mon, 34 Glasthule Road, tel. 01/284-1027). **Centra Market** is right next door and has your picnic makings (daily 7:00-23:00, Glasthule Road).

Howth

Eight miles north of Dublin, Howth rests on a teardrop-shaped peninsula that pokes the Irish Sea. Its active harbor teems with

fishing boats bringing in the daily catch and seals trolling for their scraps. Weary Dubliners come here for refreshing coastal cliff walks near the city. Located at the north terminus of the DART light rail line, Howth makes a good place for travelers to settle in, with easy connections to Dublin for sightseeing.

Howth was once an important gateway to Dublin. Near the neck of the peninsula is the suburb of Clontarf, where Irish High King Brian Boru defeated the last concerted Viking attack in 1014. Eight hundred years later, a squat martello tower was built on a bluff above Howth's harbor to defend it from a Napoleonic invasion that never came. The harbor then grew as a port for shipping from Liverpool and Wales. It was eventually eclipsed by Dun Laoghaire, which was first to gain rail access. Irish rebels smuggled German-supplied guns into Ireland via Howth in 1914, making the 1916 Easter Uprising possible. These days this hamlet is so sleepy, it didn't open a TI until 2009.

Getting to Howth

The **DART** light rail system zaps travelers between Howth and the city twice as fast as the bus and sans traffic (4/hour, 25 minutes, runs Mon-Sat about 6:00-23:30, Sun from 9:00, €2.40 one-way, €4.40 round-trips good same day only, 3-day pass-€11.80, Eurailpass valid but uses a flexi-day, tel. 01/703-3504, www.irish rail.ie). If you're coming from Dublin, catch a DART train marked

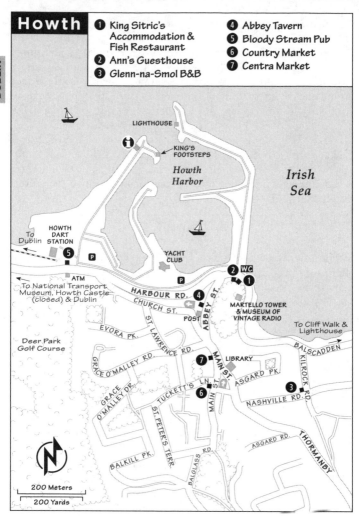

Howth

1 King Sitric's
  Accommodation &
  Fish Restaurant
2 Ann's Guesthouse
3 Glenn-na-Smol B&B

4 Abbey Tavern
5 Bloody Stream Pub
6 Country Market
7 Centra Market

LIGHTHOUSE

KING'S
FOOTSTEPS

*Howth
Harbor*

*Irish
Sea*

To
Dublin

HOWTH
DART
STATION

YACHT
CLUB

WC

ATM
To National Transport
Museum, Howth Castle
(closed) & Dublin

HARBOUR RD.

CHURCH ST.

POST

ABBEY ST.

MARTELLO TOWER
& MUSEUM OF
VINTAGE RADIO

To Cliff Walk &
Lighthouse

*Deer Park
Golf Course*

EVORA PK.

GRACE O'MALLEY RD.

ST. LAWRENCE RD.

GRACE
O'MALLEY DR.

TUCKETT'S LN.

MAIN ST.

LIBRARY

ASGARD PK.

BALSCADDEN

KILROCK RD.

NASHVILLE RD.

ST. PETER'S TERR.

BALKILL PK.

BALGLASS RD.

ASGARD RD.

THORMANBY

200 Meters
200 Yards

"Howth" (not *Howth Junction, Malahide,* or *Drogheda*) and ride it
to the end of the line—passing through Howth Junction en route.
All trains departing Howth head straight to Dublin's Connolly
Station, then continue on to Tara and Pierce stations.

If you choose to go by **bus,** #31 or #31B link Dublin's Eden
Quay and the well-marked bus stop on Howth's harborfront (1
hour, €2). A **taxi** from the airport takes about 20 minutes and
costs about €25. Try Executive Cabs (tel. 01/839-6020). With easy
DART access into Dublin and plentiful parking, Howth is a good
option for those with **cars** (which can cost more than €30/day to
park in Dublin).

Orientation to Howth

Howth perches on the north shore of the peninsula, clustered along a quarter-mile harborfront promenade that stretches from the DART station (in the west) to the martello tower on the bluff (in the east). Its two stony piers clutch like crab claws at the Irish Sea. The West Pier has the fishing action and TI, while the East Pier extends to a stubby 200-year-old lighthouse and views of a rugged nearby island, Ireland's Eye. Abbey Street extends south, uphill from the harbor near the base of the martello tower bluff, becoming Main Street with most of the shops and pubs, along with the post office (Mon-Fri 9:00-13:00 & 14:15-18:00, Sat 9:00-13:00, closed Sun) and library (free Internet access, only one terminal, Mon and Wed 14:00-20:30, Tue and Thu-Sat 10:00-13:00 & 14:00-17:00, closed Sun). Ulster Bank has the only ATM in town, across the street from the DART station and to the left of the Gem Newsstand.

Tourist Information

The TI is at the far end of the West Pier, on the ground floor of the Aqua Building (May-Oct daily 9:30-17:00, shorter hours off-season, 1 West Pier, tel. 01/839-6955, www.howthismagic.com). If the TI is closed, another good info source is your innkeeper.

Sights in Howth

Other than coastal walks, sightseeing here pales in comparison to Dublin. Nearby Howth Castle is privately owned and cannot be toured.

Museum of Vintage Radio—The three-story martello tower on the bluff overlooking the East Pier is the only sight in Howth worth a glance. Curator Pat Herbert has spent almost 50 years acquiring his collection of lovingly preserved radios, phonographs, and even a hurdy-gurdy (a crank-action musical oddity)—all of which still work. Check out the WWII-era radio disguised as a picture frame, which was used by the resistance in occupied France.

Before leaving the compact bluff, catch the views of the harbor and the nearby island of Ireland's Eye. Spot the distant martello tower on the island's west end and the white guano coating its eastern side, courtesy of a colony of gannets.

Cost and Hours: €5, May-Oct daily 11:00-16:00, Nov-April Sat-Sun only 11:00-16:00, entry up driveway off Abbey Street, www.ei0mar.org.

National Transport Museum—Housed in a large shed on the castle grounds, this is a dusty waste of time unless you find rapture in old trams and buses.

Cost and Hours: €3, June-Aug Mon-Fri 10:00-17:00, Sat-Sun 14:00-17:00, Sept-May by appointment only, tel. 01/848-0831.

St. Mary's Abbey—Looming above Abbey Street, the current ruins date from the early 1400s. Before that, a church built by Norse King Sitric in 1042 stood at this site. The entrance to the ruins is on Church Street, above the abbey grounds.

East and West Piers—The piers make for mellow strolls after a meal. Poke your head into the various fishmonger shops along the West Pier to see the day's catch. At the end of the pier (on the leeward side), you'll find the footsteps of King George IV carved into the stone after his 1821 visit. The East Pier is a quiet jetty barbed with a squat lighthouse and the closest views of Ireland's Eye. If you want to get even closer to the island, book a boat excursion (€15 round-trip, daily in summer on demand from 10:00-18:00, call for off-season trips, mobile 086-845-9154, www.islandferries .net).

Hiking Trails—Trails above the eastern cliffs of the peninsula offer enjoyable, breezy exercise. For a scenic three-hour round-trip, walk past the East Pier and martello tower, following Balscadden Road uphill. You'll soon pass Balscadden House, where writer W. B. Yeats spent part of his youth (watch for plaque on left). Where the road dead-ends, you'll find the well-marked trailhead. The trail is easy to follow, and soon you'll be walking south around the craggy coastline to grand views of the Bailey Lighthouse on the southeast rim of the peninsula. The gate to the lighthouse grounds is always locked, so enjoy the view from afar before retracing your steps back to Howth.

Sleeping in Howth

(€1 = about $1.40, country code: 353, area code: 01)

$$$ King Sitric's Accommodation is Howth's best lodging option and has a fine harborfront seafood restaurant (described below). It fills the old harbormaster's house with eight well-kept rooms and a friendly staff (Sb-€110-145, Db-€150-205, Tb-€190-245, discounts for 2-night stay, online deals, non-smoking, Wi-Fi, East Pier below martello tower, tel. 01/832-5235, fax 01/839-2442, www .kingsitric.ie, info@kingsitric.ie, Aidan and Joan MacManus).

$ Ann's Guesthouse, next door to King Sitric's, sports four bright, airy rooms on its top floor—two with skylight views of the harbor (Sb/Db-€80, 5 East Pier, tel. 01/832-3197, www.annsof howth.com, jonathancooke.cooke@gmail.com, Jon Cooke).

$ Glenn-na-Smol B&B is a homey house with six unpretentious rooms in a quiet setting, a 10-minute walk uphill along the coast behind the martello tower (Sb-€40, Db-€70, Tb-€90, Qb-€100, cash only, Wi-Fi, parking, corner of Nashville Road

& Kilrock Road, tel. 01/832-2936, rickards@indigo.ie, Sean and Kitty Rickard).

Eating in Howth

DUBLIN

King Sitric's Fish Restaurant, one of the area's most famous sea-food experiences, serves Irish versions of French classics in a dining room (upstairs) with harbor views. Chef Aidan MacManus rises early each morning to select the best of the day's catch on the pier, to be enjoyed that evening by happy customers (€22-30 meals, Mon and Wed-Sat 18:30-22:00, Sun 13:00-19:00, closed Tue, reservations smart, tel. 01/832-5235, www.kingsitric.ie).

For pub grub, try the **Abbey Tavern** up the hill on Abbey Street (occasional trad music and dance, call for schedule, tel. 01/839-0307 or 01/832-2006). Another good choice is the **Bloody Stream Pub** in front of the DART station (tel. 01/839-5076). The **Country Market** sells picnic supplies, and its cheap and friendly upstairs tea room offers lunch (Mon-Sat 7:00-19:00, Sun 7:00-17:00, Main Street). The **Centra Market** is a block closer to the waterfront (daily 7:00-22:00, Main Street).

NEAR DUBLIN

Brú na Bóinne • Trim • Glendalough •
Wicklow Mountains • Irish National Stud

Not far from urban Dublin, the stony skeletons of evocative ruins sprout from the lush Irish countryside. The story of Irish history is told by ancient burial mounds, early Christian monastic settlements, huge Norman castles, and pampered estate gardens. In gentler inland terrain, the Irish love of equestrian sport is nurtured in grassy pastures ruled by spirited thoroughbreds. These sights are separated into three regions: north of Dublin (the Valley of the Boyne, including Brú na Bóinne and the town of Trim), south of Dublin (Powerscourt Gardens, Glendalough, and the Wicklow Mountains), and west of Dublin (the Irish National Stud).

North of Dublin: The Valley of the Boyne

The peaceful, green Valley of the Boyne, just 30 miles north of Dublin, has an impressive concentration of historical and spiritual sights: The enigmatic burial mounds at Brú na Bóinne are older than the Egyptian pyramids. At the Hill of Tara (seat of the high kings of Celtic Ireland), St. Patrick preached his most persuasive sermon. The valley also contains the first monastery in Ireland built in the style used on the Continent, and several of the country's finest high crosses. You'll see Trim's 13th-century castle—Ireland's biggest—built by Norman invaders, and you can wander the site of the historic Battle of the Boyne (1690), in which the Protestants turned the tide against the

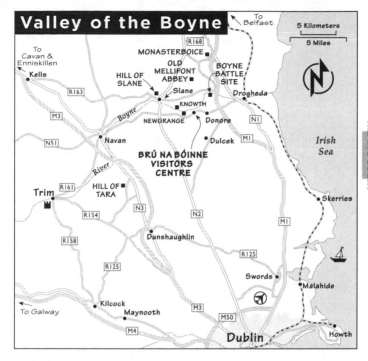

Catholics and imposed British rule until the 20th century.

Planning Your Time

Of these sights, only Brú na Bóinne is worth ▲▲▲ (and deserves a good three hours). The others, while relatively meager physically, are powerfully evocative to anyone interested in Irish history and culture. Without a car, I'd visit only Brú na Bóinne, taking the shuttle bus from Dublin.

The region is a joy by car, because all of the described sights are within a 30-minute drive of each other. If you eat your Weetabix and get an early start, you could do the entire region in a day. Though the sights are on tiny roads, they're well-marked with brown, tourist-friendly road signs. You'll navigate best using an Ordnance Survey atlas.

As you plan your Ireland itinerary, if you're flying into or out of Dublin, and want to avoid the intensity and expense of that big city, consider using Trim as an overnight base (45-minute drive from airport) and tour these sights from there.

Tours of the Valley of the Boyne

If you lack a car and like tours, consider one of these round-trip excursions from Dublin.

Mary Gibbon's Tours visits the Brú na Bóinne (including inside the Newgrange tomb), the Hill of Tara, and the Hill of Slane in a six-hour trip (€35, Mon-Fri only, 9:30 pickup at Mespil Hotel at 50-60 Mespil Road, 10:15 pickup at Dublin TI on Suffolk Street, 10:25 pickup at AIB Bank at 37-38 Upper O'Connell Street, home by 16:30, book direct rather than through TI, mobile 086-355-1355, www.newgrangetours.com, info@newgrangetours.com).

Over the Top Tours leaves Dublin at 9:00 and returns by 17:30, with stops at the Hill of Tara, the Hill of Slane (free time for lunch), Fourknocks (prehistoric tombs, less famous and less crowded than Brú na Bóinne), and the monasteries of Monasterboice and Old Mellifont Abbey (€29, daily, 9:00 pickup at Gresham Hotel on Upper O'Connell Street, 9:20 pickup at Dublin TI on Suffolk Street, 14-seat minibus, reservations required, hold seat by leaving credit-card number, Ireland toll-free tel. 1-800-424-252, Dublin tel. 01/860-0404, mobile 087-259-3467, www.overthetoptours.com, info@overthetoptours.com).

Brú na Bóinne

The famous archaeological site properly known as Brú na Bóinne—"dwelling place of the Boyne"—is also commonly referred to as "Newgrange" (although that's actually the name of one of the tombs). The well-organized site, worth ▲▲▲, centers on a state-of-the-art museum and visitors center. You'll receive an appointment for a shuttle bus that ferries small groups five minutes away to one of two 5,000-year-old passage tombs, where a guide gives a 30-minute tour.

The **Newgrange** tomb is more famous, and allows you inside. **Knowth** (rhymes with "south") opened more recently and is more extensive, but you can't go inside the tomb. At the center, you'll buy a ticket to one or both sights, and be given bus departure times (if you plan to see both sights, note that buses depart 1.5 hours apart). Newgrange sells out first, and it comes with a longer wait. If you opt for Knowth, be sure to see the museum's replica of the Newgrange passage entrance (where a short tour and winter solstice light-show demo often occur upon request); the replica is connected to the video room. Each site is different enough and worthwhile, but for many, seeing just one is adequate..

Warning for Drivers: If you've using a modern GPS system, input "Brú na Bóinne" into your system rather than "Newgrange" or you'll end up at the actual Newgrange burial mound (with no ticket booths or access into the site). You must first go to the Brú na Bóinne Visitors Centre two miles (3.2 km) away, and then ride a shuttle bus to the tomb.

Newgrange is one single mound and is the more restored of the Brú na Bóinne sites. Dating from 3200 B.C., it's 500 years older than the pyramids at Giza. While we know nothing of the builders, it most certainly was a sacred spot that was devoted to some kind of Sun God ritual. During the tour, you'll squeeze down a narrow passageway to a cross-shaped central chamber located under a 20-foot-high igloo-type stone dome. Bones and ashes were placed here under 200,000 tons of stone and dirt to wait for a special moment. As the sun rose on the shortest day of the year (winter solstice, Dec 21), a ray of light crept slowly down the 60-foot-long passageway. For 17 minutes, it lit the center of the sacred chamber. Perhaps this was the moment when the souls of the dead were transported to the afterlife, via that mysterious ray of life-giving and life-taking light.

Knowth (the second Brú na Bóinne site) is a necropolis of several grassy mounds around one 85-yard-wide grand tomb. The big mound, covering 1.5 acres, has two passages aligned so that on the spring and fall equinoxes, rays from the rising and setting sun shine down the passageways to the center chamber. Neither of the passages is open to the public, but when you visit a room cut into the mound—designed to expose the interior construction layers—you get a glimpse down one of the passages. The Knowth site thrived from 3000 to 2000 B.C., with mysterious burial rituals and sun-tracking ceremonies to please the gods and ensure the regular progression of seasons for crops. The site then evolved into the domain of fairies and myths for the next 2,000 years, and became an Iron Age fortress in the early centuries after Christ. Around A.D. 1000, it was an all-Ireland political center, and, later, a Norman fortress was built atop the mound. You'll see plenty of mysteriously carved stones and new-feeling grassy mounds that you can look down on from atop the grand tomb.

Cost and Hours: The museum in the Brú na Bóinne Visitors Centre is included in the prices for the tombs: Newgrange-€6, Knowth-€5. The site is open May-Sept daily 9:00-18:30, slightly shorter hours off-season, last entry to visitors center is 45 minutes before closing. Newgrange is open year-round, while Knowth is open Easter-Oct only. Allow an hour for the excellent museum and an hour for each of the tombs. Tel. 041/988-0300, www.worldheritageireland.ie.

Crowd-Beating Tips: Visits are limited, and on busy summer days those arriving in the afternoon may not get a spot on a shuttle bus (no reservations possible). In peak season, try to arrive before 10:00 to avoid a wait caused by the big, tour-bus day-trip crowds from Dublin. Upon arrival you'll generally get a bus departure time for one or both of the passage-tomb sites (the last bus leaves 1.75 hours before closing). Spend your wait-time visiting the museum, watching the great seven-minute video, and munching lunch in the cheery cafeteria. You can't drive directly to the actual passage tombs.

Getting There: To reach the Brú na Bóinne Visitors Centre from Dublin by **car**, drive north on N1 to Drogheda, where signs direct you to the visitors center. To better understand the layout of this site and shuttle-bus route, spend a moment studying the helpful aerial-view panels by the stone pathway that leads from the parking lot to the visitors center.

If you don't have a car and you're not taking a day tour, hop on the **Newgrange shuttle bus,** a handy service that runs from Dublin directly to the visitors center (€17 round-trip, 45 minutes, must book in advance, departs at 8:45 and 11:15 from Gresham Hotel on Upper O'Connell Street, and at 9:00 and 11:30 from Dublin TI on Suffolk Street, return trips depart at 13:30 and 16:30 from the visitors center, run by Over the Top Tours, book by calling 01/860-0405 or 1-800-424-252, www.overthetoptours.com).

More Sights in the Valley of the Boyne

▲▲Battle of the Boyne Site

One of Europe's lesser-known battlegrounds (but huge in Irish history), this is the pastoral riverside site of the pivotal battle in which the Protestant British broke Catholic resistance, establishing Protestant rule over all Ireland and Britain.

It was here in 1690 that Protestant King William III, with his English/Irish/Dutch/Danish/French Huguenot army, defeated his father-in-law—who was also his uncle—Catholic King James II and his Irish/French army. King William's forces, on the north side of the Boyne, managed to fight their way across the river, and by the end of the day, King James was fleeing south in full retreat. He soon left Ireland, but his forces fought on until their final defeat a year later. James the Second (called "James da Turd" by those who scorn his lack of courage and leadership) never returned, and he died a bitter ex-monarch in France. King William of Orange's victory, on the other hand, is still celebrated in Northern Ireland every July 12, with controversial marches by Unionist "Orangemen."

The 50,000 soldiers who fought here made this the largest battle ever to take place in the British Isles. Yet it was only a side skirmish in an even larger continental confrontation pitting France's King Louis XIV against the "Grand Alliance" of nations threatened by France's dominant military and frequent incursions into neighboring lands.

Louis ruled by divine right, answerable only to God—and James modeled himself after Louis. Even the Pope (who could control neither Louis nor James and was equally disturbed by Catholic France's aggressions) backed Protestant King William against Catholic King James—just one example of the pretzel logic that was the European mind-set at the time.

The site of the Battle of the Boyne was bought in 1997 by the Irish Office of Public Works, part of the Republic's governmental efforts to honor a place sacred to Unionists in Northern Ireland—despite the fact that the battle's outcome ensured Catholic subordination to the Protestant minority for the next 230 years.

The **Visitors Centre** is housed in a mansion built on the battlefield 50 years after the conflict. The exhibits do a good job illustrating the international nature of the battle and its place in the wider context of European political power struggles. The highlight is a huge battleground model with laser lights that move troops around the terrain, showing the battle's ebb and flow on that bloody day. A separate 15-minute film (shown in the former stable house) runs continuously and does a fine job of fleshing out the battle.

The Saturday and Sunday afternoon **"Living History" demonstrations** in summer are a treat for history buffs and photographers, with guides clad in 17th-century garb. You'll get a bang out of the musket loading and firing demo (at 11:00, 13:00, 15:00, and 17:00), see cavalry combat in full gallop (at 12:00, 14:00, and 16:00), and learn that the plight of an Irish watermelon is to fear the sword.

Cost and Hours: €4, daily May-Sept 10:00-18:00, March-April 9:30-17:30, Oct-Feb 9:00-17:00, last admission one hour before closing, tea room/cafeteria, tel. 041/980-9950, www.battle oftheboyne.ie.

▲Hill of Tara

This was the most important center of political and religious power in pre-Christian Ireland. While aerial views show plenty of mysterious circles and lines, wandering with the sheep among the well-worn ditches and hills leaves you with more to feel than to see. Visits are made meaningful by an excellent 20-minute video presentation and the caring 20-minute guided walk that follows (always available upon request and entirely worthwhile).

You'll see the Mound of Hostages (a Bronze Age passage grave, c. 2500 B.C.), a couple of ancient sacred stones, a war memorial, and vast views over the Emerald Isle. While ancient Ireland was a pig pile of minor chieftain-kings scrambling for power, the high king of Tara was king of the mountain. It was at this ancient stockade that St. Patrick directly challenged the king's authority. When confronted by the high king, Patrick convincingly explained the Holy Trinity using a shamrock: three petals with one stem. He won the right to preach Christianity throughout Ireland, and the country had a new national symbol.

This now-desolate hill was also the scene of great modern events. In 1798, passionate young Irish rebels chose Tara for its defensible position, but were routed by better organized (and more sober) British troops. (The cunning British commander had sent three cartloads of whiskey along the nearby road earlier in the day, knowing the rebels would intercept it.) In 1843, the great orator and champion of Irish liberty Daniel O'Connell gathered 500,000 Irish peasants on this hill for his greatest "monster meeting"—a peaceful show of force demanding the repeal of the Act of Union with Britain (kind of the Woodstock of its day). In a bizarre final twist, a small group of British Israelites—who believed they were one of the lost tribes of Israel, who had ended up in Britain—spent 1899 to 1901 recklessly digging up parts of the hill in a misguided search for the Ark of the Covenant.

Stand on the Hill of Tara. Think of the history it's seen, and survey Ireland. It's understandable why this "meeting place of heroes" continues to hold a powerful place in the Irish psyche.

Cost and Hours: €3, includes video and 20-minute guided walk, mid-May-mid-Sept daily 10:00-18:00, last tour at 17:00; otherwise, access to site is free but visitors center is closed; tel. 046/902-5903. Wear good walking shoes—the ground is uneven and often wet

Old Mellifont Abbey

This Cistercian abbey (the first in Ireland) was established by French monks who came to the country in 1142 to bring the Irish monks more in line with Rome. (Even the abbey's architecture was unusual, marking the first time in Ireland that a formal, European-style monastic layout was used.) Cistercians lived isolated rural lives; lay monks worked the land, allowing the more educated monks to devote all their energy to prayer. After Henry VIII dissolved the abbey in 1539, centuries of locals used it as a handy quarry. Consequently, little survives beyond the octagonal lavabo, where the monks would ceremonially wash their hands before entering the refectory to eat. The lavabo gives a sense of the abbey's former grandeur. The excellent 45-minute tours, available upon request and included in your admission, give meaning to the site.

Cost and Hours: €3, May-Sept daily 10:00-18:00, last tour at 16:30, no tours Oct-April when site is free and you can explore on your own, tel. 041/982-6459, www.heritageireland.ie.

Monasterboice

This ruined monastery is visit-worthy for its round tower and its ornately carved high crosses—two of the best such crosses in Ireland. In the Dark Ages, these crosses, illustrated from top to bottom with Bible stories, gave monks a teaching tool as they preached to the illiterate masses. Imagine the crosses in their heyday, when they were brightly painted (before years of wind and rain weathered the paint away). Today, Monasterboice is basically an old graveyard.

The 18-foot-tall **Cross of Murdock** (Muiredach's Cross, A.D. 923, named after an abbot) is considered the best high cross in Ireland. The circle—which characterizes the Irish high cross—could represent the perfection of God. Or, to help ease pagans into Christianity, it may represent the sun, which was worshipped in pre-Christian Celtic society. Whatever its symbolic purpose was, its practical function was to support the weight of the crossbeam.

Face the cross (with the round tower in the background) and study the carved sandstone. The center panel shows the Last Judgment, with Christ under a dove, symbolizing the Holy Spirit. Those going to heaven are on Christ's right, and the damned are being ushered away by a pitchfork-wielding devil on his

left. Working down, you'll see the Archangel Michael weighing souls, as the Devil tugs demonically at the scales; the adoration of the three—or four—Magi; Moses striking the rock to bring forth water; scenes from the life of David; and, finally, Adam, Eve, and the apple next to Cain slaying Abel. Imagine these carvings with their original, colorful paint jobs. Check out the plaque at the base of the nearby tree, which further explains the carvings on the cross.

Find the even-taller cross nearest the tower. It seems the top section was broken off and buried for a period, which protected it from weathering. The bottom part remained standing, enduring the erosive effect of Irish weather, which smeared the once-crisp features.

The door to the round tower was originally 15-20 feet above

the ground (accessible by ladder). After centuries of burials, the ground level has risen.

Cost and Hours: Free and always open.

Trim

The sleepy, workaday town of Trim, straddling the River Boyne, is marked by the towering ruins of Trim Castle. Trim feels littered with mighty ruins that seem to say, "This little town was big-time...700 years ago." The tall Yellow Steeple (over the river from the castle) is all that remains of the 14th-century Augustinian Abbey of St. Mary. Not far away, the Sheep's Gate is a humble remnant of the once-grand medieval town walls. A pleasant half-mile walk back toward Dublin takes you to the sprawling ruins of Saints Peter and Paul Cathedral (from 1206), once the largest Gothic church in Ireland. Across the 15th-century Norman bridge from the cathedral are the 13th-century ruins of the Hospital of St. John the Baptist. Near the town center, the modest, 30-foot-tall Wellington Column honors native son Arthur Wellesley, the First Duke of Wellington (1769-1852), who spent his childhood in Trim and twice became prime minister.

If you're flying into or out of Dublin Airport and don't want to deal with big-city Dublin, Trim is a perfect alternative—an easy 45-minute, 30-mile drive away. You can rent a car at the airport and make Trim your first overnight base (getting used to driving on the other side of the road in easier country traffic), or spend your last night here before returning your car at the airport. Either way, you don't need or want a car in Dublin, where parking is expensive and sightseeing is best on foot, or by bus or taxi.

Orientation to Trim

(area code: 046)
Trim's main square is a traffic roundabout, and everything's within a block or two. Most of the shops and eateries are on or near Market Street, along with banks and a supermarket.

Tourist Information

The TI is right next to the castle entrance and includes a handy coffee shop. Drop in for a free map and to check out the collage of photos in the entryway, showing the castle dolled up for the filming of *Braveheart* (June-Aug Mon-Fri 9:30-17:30, Sat-Sun 12:00-17:30, shorter hours Sept-May, Castle Street, tel. 046/943-7227).

The TI organizes historical walking tours of the town, led by enthusiastic volunteers (€5, pay at TI, daily at 14:30 and 19:00, 1 hour; tours depart from the bog oak sculpture—facing the TI, go

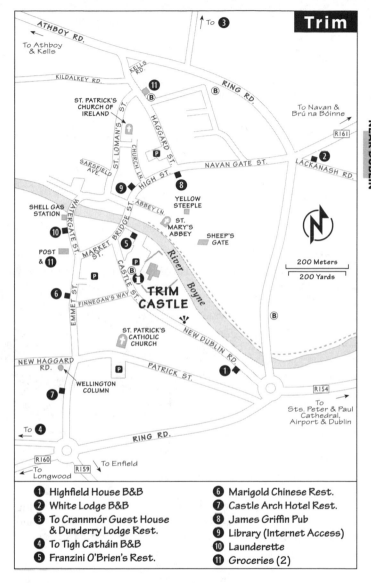

NEAR DUBLIN

1 Highfield House B&B
2 White Lodge B&B
3 To Crannmór Guest House & Dunderry Lodge Rest.
4 To Tigh Catháin B&B
5 Franzini O'Brien's Rest.
6 Marigold Chinese Rest.
7 Castle Arch Hotel Rest.
8 James Griffin Pub
9 Library (Internet Access)
10 Launderette
11 Groceries (2)

100 feet down sidewalk to right; tel. 046/943-7227).

Helpful Hints

Internet Access: The **library** offers 30 minutes of free Internet access (Tue and Thu 10:00-20:30, Wed and Fri-Sat 10:00-13:00 & 14:00-17:00, closed Sun-Mon, High Street).

Post Office: It's tucked in the back of the **Spar Market** (Mon-Fri

9:00-17:30, Sat 9:00-13:00, closed Sun, Emmett Street).

Laundry: The launderette is located close to Market Street (Mon-Sat 9:00-13:00 & 14:00-17:30, closed Sun, Watergate Street, tel. 046/943-7176).

Parking: To park on the street or in a public lot, use the pay-and-display parking system. Buy a ticket at machines spaced along the street, and display it on your dashboard (Mon-Sat 9:00-18:00, €0.90/hour, 2-hour max, free Sun).

Fishing Tours: Marc O'Regan leads backcountry trout and pike fishing trips, making a splash with anglers who want to experience Ireland's bountiful lakes and rivers (tel. 046/943-1635, www.crannmor.com). O'Regan and his wife also run the recommended Crannmór Guest House.

Sights in Trim

▲▲**Trim Castle**—This is the biggest Norman castle in Ireland. Set in a grassy riverside park at the edge of this sleepy town, its mighty keep towers above a very ruined outer wall. The current castle was

completed in the 1220s and served as a powerful Norman statement to the restless Irish natives. It remains an impressive sight—so impressive that it was used in the 1994 filming of *Braveheart* (which was actually about Scotland's—not Ireland's—fight for freedom from the English).

The best-preserved walls ring the castle's southern perimeter and sport a barbican gate that contained two drawbridges. At the base of the castle walls, notice the cleverly angled "batter" wall—used by defenders who hurled down stones that banked off at great velocity into the attacking army. Notice also that the castle is built directly on bedrock, visible along the base of the walls. During sieges, while defenders of other castles feared that attackers would tunnel underground to weaken the defensive walls, that was not an issue here.

The massive 70-foot-high central keep, which is mostly a hollow shell, has 20 sides. This experimental design was not implemented elsewhere because it increased the number of defenders needed to cover all the angles. You can go inside the keep only with the included tour, where you'll start by checking out the cool ground-floor models showing the evolution of the castle. Then you'll climb a series of tightly winding original staircases and modern, high catwalks, learn about life in the castle, and end at the top with great views of the walls and the countryside.

Make time to take a 15-minute walk outside, circling the castle walls and stopping at the informative plaques that show the castle from each viewpoint during its gory glory days. Night strollers are treated to views of the castle hauntingly lit in blue-green hues.

Cost and Hours: €3 for castle grounds, €4 for entrance to keep and required tour; roughly April-Oct daily 10:00-18:00; Nov-March Sat-Sun only 10:00-17:00, closed Mon-Fri; last entry one hour before closing; 45-minute tours run 2/hour but spots are limited, so arrive early in peak season as tours can fill up; tel. 046/943-8619, www.heritageireland.ie.

The Power & Glory—This grade-schoolish, 30-minute slideshow overview of the personalities and history of the castle is followed by an exhibit on life here in Norman times. The show and a cup of coffee help to pass the time as you wait for your castle tour.

Cost and Hours: €3, Mon-Sat 9:30-17:30, Sun 12:00-17:00, shorter hours off-season, show runs on demand, in visitors center with TI next to castle, Castle Street, tel. 046/943-7227.

Sleeping in Trim

$$ Highfield House B&B, across the street from the castle and a five-minute walk from town, is a stately 180-year-old former maternity hospital, with hardwood floors and nine spacious, high-ceilinged rooms (Sb-€50-55, Db-€78-84, Tb-€99-110, nonsmoking rooms, family-friendly, free Internet access and Wi-Fi; overlooks roundabout where Dublin Road hits Trim, just before castle at Castle Street; tel. 046/943-6386, www.highfieldguesthouse.com, highfieldhouseaccom@eircom.net, Geraldine and

---

Sleep Code

(€1 = about $1.40, country code: 353, area code: 046)
S = Single, **D** = Double/Twin, **T** = Triple, **Q** = Quad, **b** = bathroom, **s** = shower only. Credit cards are accepted and breakfast is included unless otherwise noted.

To help you easily sort through these listings, I've divided the accommodations into two categories, based on the price for a standard double room with bath:

$$ Higher Priced—Most rooms more than €70.
$ Lower Priced—Most rooms €70 or less.

Prices can change without notice; verify the hotel's current rates online or by email. For other updates, see www.ricksteves.com/update.

Edward Duignan).

$ White Lodge B&B, a 10-minute walk northwest of the castle, has six comfortably unpretentious rooms with an oak-and-granite lounge (Sb-€45, Db-€68, Tb-€76, Qb-€84, 10 percent discount for active-duty members of the US and Canadian armed forces with this book, free Internet access and Wi-Fi, parking, New Road, tel. 046/943-6549, www.whitelodgetrim.com, whitelodgetrim@eircom.net, Todd O'Loughlin). They also offer a family-friendly self-catering house next door.

Countryside B&Bs

These two B&Bs are in the quiet countryside about a mile outside Trim (phone ahead for driving directions).

At **$$ Crannmór Guest House,** north of town, Anne O'Regan decorates five rooms with cheery color schemes (Sb-€45-55, Db-€76-80, Tb-€90, Qb-€110, Wi-Fi, Dunderry Road, tel. 046/943-1635, mobile 087-288-7390, fax 046/943-8087, www.crannmor.com, cranmor@eircom.net). Her professional-guide husband Marc knows all the best fishing holes.

Mrs. Keane's **$$ Tigh Catháin B&B,** southwest of town, has four large, bright, lacy rooms with a comfy, rural feel (Db-€70-75, Tb-€85-95, cash only, Wi-Fi, on R160/Longwood Road, tel. 046/943-1996, mobile 086-257-7313, www.tighcathain-bnb.com, marie@tighcathain-bnb.com).

Eating in Trim

A country-market town, Trim offers basic meat-and-potatoes lunch and dinner options. Don't waste time searching here for gourmet food. The restaurants and cafés along Market Street are friendly, wholesome, and unassuming (soup-and-sandwich delis close at 17:30).

Franzini O'Brien's is the only place in town with a fun dinner menu and enough business to make it work. They serve pasta, steak, fish, and good salads in a modern, candlelit ambience. Nothing's Irish except the waiters (€15-26 dishes, €20 two-course or €25 three-course early-bird dinners before 19:30, Mon-Sat 17:00-22:00, Sun 13:00-21:00, French's Lane across from the castle parking lot, tel. 046/943-1002).

If you feel like having Chinese food, **Marigold** fits the bill (Mon-Sat 17:00-23:00, Sun 16:00-23:00, Emmett Street, tel. 046/943-8788).

For a tasty splurge of gourmet cooking out in the country, get driving directions to **Dunderry Lodge,** four miles (6.4 km) north of Trim off the Dunderry Road (€20 early-bird dinner Mon-Fri 17:30-19:00, Mon-Sat 19:30-21:30, Sun 12:30-14:30 & 18:30-20:30, tel. 046/943-1671).

The **Castle Arch Hotel,** popular with locals, serves hearty pub grub at reasonable prices in its bistro (€11-14 meals, daily 12:30-21:30, tel. 046/943-1516).

For a fun pub experience, check out Trim's best watering hole, the **James Griffin** (on High Street). It's full of local characters and old-fashioned atmosphere, with traditional Irish music sessions on Monday and Wednesday nights.

Supermarkets: **Spar Market** has everything you need to create a picnic (Mon-Fri 7:30-21:00, Sat-Sun 8:00-21:00, Emmett Street). The same goes for **Super Valu,** a larger store on Haggard Street that's a bit farther from the town center (daily 8:00-22:00).

Trim Connections

Trim has no train station; the nearest is in Drogheda 25 miles away on the coast. Buses from Trim to **Dublin** (almost hourly, 1 hour) pick you up at the bus shelter next to the TI and castle entrance on Castle Street. For details, see www.buseireann.ie.

South of Dublin: Glendalough and the Wicklow Mountains

The Wicklow Mountains, while only 10 miles south of Dublin, feel remote—enough so to have provided a handy refuge for opponents to English rule. Rebels who took part in the 1798 Irish uprising hid out here for years. When the frustrated British built a military road in 1800 to help flush out the rebels, the area became more accessible. Today, this same road—now R115—takes you through the Wicklow area to Glendalough at its south end. While the valley is the darling of the Dublin day-trip tour organizers, it doesn't live up to the hype. But two blockbuster sights—Glendalough and the Gardens of Powerscourt—make a visit worth considering.

Getting Around

By car or tour, it's easy. If you lack wheels, take a tour. It's not worth the trouble on public transport.

By Car: It's a delight. Take N11 south from Dublin toward Bray, then R117 to Enniskerry, the gateway to the Wicklow Mountains. Signs direct you to the gardens and on to Glendalough. From Glendalough, if you're heading west, you can leave the val-

NEAR DUBLIN

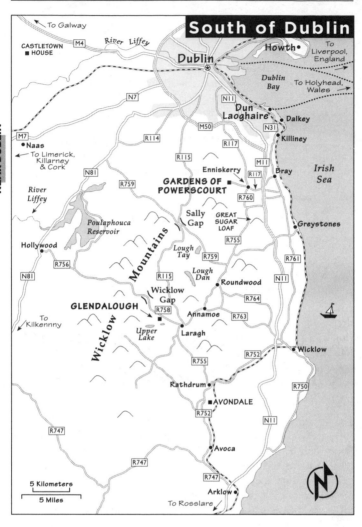

South of Dublin

To Galway
CASTLETOWN HOUSE
M4
River Liffey
Dublin
Howth
To Liverpool, England
N7
Dublin Bay
To Holyhead, Wales
N11
Dun Laoghaire
Dalkey
N31
M50
Killiney
M7
R114
R117
M11
Naas
To Limerick, Killarney & Cork
N81
R115
Enniskerry
R117
Bray
Irish Sea
River Liffey
R759
GARDENS OF POWERSCOURT
R760
Poulaphouca Reservoir
Sally Gap
GREAT SUGAR LOAF
R755
Greystones
Hollywood
R756
Lough Tay
R759
R761
N81
Mountains
R115
Lough Dan
Roundwood
N11
Wicklow Gap
R764
GLENDALOUGH
R758
Annamoe
R763
To Kilkennny
Wicklow
Upper Lake
Laragh
R755
R752
Wicklow
Rathdrum
R750
R752
AVONDALE
N11
R747
Avoca
R747
5 Kilometers
5 Miles
R747
Arklow
To Rosslare

ley (and pick up the highway to the west) over the famous but dull mountain pass called the Wicklow Gap.

By Tour from Dublin: Wild Wicklow Tours covers the region with an entertaining guide who packs every minute with information and *craic* (interesting, fun conversation). With a gang of 40 packed into tight but comfortable mountain-gripping buses, the guide kicks into gear from the first pickup in Dublin. Tours cover Dublin's embassy row, Dun Laoghaire, the Bay of Dublin (with the mansions of Ireland's rich and famous), the windy military road over scenic Sally Gap, and the Glendalough monasteries (€28, €25 for students and readers with this book in 2012, daily year-round, 9:10 pickup at Dublin TI on Suffolk Street, 10:00 pickup at Dun Laoghaire TI at ferry terminal, stop for lunch at a pub—cost not included, return through Dun Laoghaire and on to Dublin by 17:30, Dun Laoghaire-ites could stay on the bus to continue into Dublin for the evening, advance booking required, tel. 01/280-1899, www.wildwicklow.ie).

Over the Top Tours bypasses mansions and gardens to focus on Wicklow scenery. Stops include Glendalough, Sally Gap, the Glenmacnass waterfall, and Blessington lakes (€28, 9:20 pickup at Gresham Hotel on Upper O'Connell Street, 9:45 pickup at Dublin TI on Suffolk Street, return by 17:30, 14-seat minibus, reservations required, hold seat by leaving credit-card number, Ireland toll-free tel. 1-800-424-252, Dublin tel. 01/860-0404, mobile 087-259-3467, www.overthetoptours.com, info@overthetoptours.com).

Sights in the Wicklow Area

▲▲Gardens of Powerscourt

A mile above the village of Enniskerry, the Gardens of Powerscourt cover several thousand acres within the 16,000-acre estate. The dreamy driveway alone is a mile long. While the mansion's interior, only partially restored after a 1974 fire, isn't much, its meticulously kept aristocratic gardens are Ireland's best. The house was

commissioned in the 1730s by Richard Wingfield, first viscount of Powerscourt. The gardens, created during the Victorian era (1858-1875), are called "the grand finale of Europe's formal gardening tradition... probably the last garden of its size and quality ever to be created." I'll buy that.

Upon entry, you'll get a flier laying out 40-minute and one-hour walks. The "one-hour" walk takes 30 minutes at a slow amble. With the impressive summit of the Great Sugar Loaf Mountain as a backdrop, and a fine Japanese garden, Italian garden, and goofy pet cemetery along the way, this attraction provides the scenic greenery I hoped to find in the rest of the Wicklow area. The lush movies *Barry Lyndon* and *The Count of Monte Cristo* were filmed in this well-watered aristocratic fantasy.

Cost and Hours: €8, daily May-Aug 9:30-19:00, April and Sept-Oct 10:30-17:30, Nov-March 10:30-16:00, great cafeteria, tel. 01/204-6000, www.powerscourt.ie. Skip the associated waterfall (€5, 4 miles/6.5 km away).

Sleeping in Enniskerry: Drivers coming straight from Dublin Airport can stay overnight in Enniskerry at the nearby **$$ Brook**

Cottage B&B, a quiet guesthouse that's popular with hikers. It has a rambling floor plan and sports six rooms, two friendly greyhounds, comfortable beds, and traditional breakfasts in a country setting (Sb-€50-60, Db-€80, Tb-€105, cash only, 10 percent discount for multiple-night stays, Wi-Fi; from Enniskerry clock tower go 1.8 miles/3 km up Kilgarron Hill toward Glencree, look for B&B sign on the right, follow arrow sign on right side of road to end of narrow lane on left side of road, and pass through green gates; tel. 01/276-6039, mobile 086-824-1687, www.enniskerry.org, brookcottagebb@eircom.net, Mary and Jeff Drexler).

▲Military Road over Sally Gap

This trip is only for those with a car. From the Gardens of Powerscourt and Enniskerry, go to Glencree, where you drive the tiny military road over Sally Gap and through the best scenery of the Wicklow Mountains (on Sundays, watch for dozens of bicycle racers). Look for the German military cemetery, built for U-boat sailors who washed ashore in World War II. Near Sally Gap, notice the peat bogs and the freshly cut peat bricks drying in the wind. Many locals are nostalgic for the "good old days," when homes were always peat-fire heated. At the Sally Gap junction, turn left, where a road winds through the vast Guinness estate. Look down on the glacial lake (Lough Tay) and the Guinness mansion (famous for jet-set parties). Nicknamed "Guinness Lake," the water looks like Ireland's favorite dark-brown stout, and the sand of the beach actually looks like the head of a Guinness beer. From here, the road meanders scenically down into the village of Roundwood and on to Glendalough.

▲▲Glendalough

The steep wooded slopes of Glendalough (GLEN-da-lock, "Valley of the Two Lakes"), at the south end of Wicklow's military road, hide Ireland's most impressive monastic settlement. Founded by St. Kevin in the sixth century, the monastery flourished (despite repeated Viking raids) throughout the Age of Saints and Scholars until the English destroyed it in 1398. Though it was finally abandoned during the Dissolution of the Monasteries in 1539, pilgrims kept coming, especially on St. Kevin's Day, June 3. (This might have something to do with the fact that a pope said seven visits to Glendalough had the same indulgence—or forgiveness from sins—value as one visit to Rome.) While much restoration was done in the 1870s, most of the buildings date from the 10th-12th centuries.

The valley sights are split between the two lakes. The lower lake has the visitors center and the best buildings. The upper lake has scant ruins and feels like a state park, with a grassy lakeside picnic area and school groups. Walkers and hikers will enjoy a choice of nine different trails of varying lengths through the lush Wicklow countryside (longest loop takes four hours, hiking-trail maps available at visitors center).

Planning Your Time: Park for free at the Glendalough Visitors Centre. Visit the center, wander the ruins (free) around the round tower, walk the traffic-free Green Road one mile to the upper lake, and then walk back to your car. Or you can drive to the upper lake (more free parking—except July-Aug, when it's €4). If you're rushed, skip the upper lake. Summer tour-bus crowds are terrible all day on weekends and 11:00-14:00 on weekdays.

Glendalough Visitor Centre: Start your visit here (€3, daily mid-March–mid-Oct 9:30-18:00, mid-Oct–mid-March 9:30-17:00, last entry 45 minutes before closing, tel. 0404/45352). The 20-minute video provides a good thumbnail background on monastic society in medieval Ireland. While the video is more general than specific to Glendalough, the adjacent museum room does feature this particular monastic settlement. The model in the center of the room re-creates the fortified village of the year 1050. A browse through the interactive exhibits here shows the contribution these monks made to intellectual life in Dark Age Europe (such as illuminated manuscripts and Irish minuscule, a more compact alphabet developed in the seventh century).

From the Visitor Centre, a short and scenic walk along the Green Road takes you to the round tower.

The Monastic Village: Easily the best ruins of Glendalough gather around the famous 110-foot-tall round tower. Towers like this (usually 60-110 feet tall) were standard features in such settlements, functioning as bell towers, storage lofts, beacons for pilgrims, and last-resort refuges during Viking raids (though given enough warning, monks were safer hiding in the surrounding forest). The towers had a high door with a pull-up ladder—both for safety and because a door at ground level would have weakened the tower's foundation. Several ruined churches (10th-12th centuries) and a sea of grave markers complete this evocative scene. Markers give short descriptions of the ruined buildings.

In an Ireland without cities, these monastic communities were mainstays of civilization. They were remote outposts where ascetics (with a taste for scenic settings) gathered to commune with God. In the 12th century, with the arrival of grander monastic orders such as the Franciscans and the

Dominicans and with the growth of cities, these monastic communities were eclipsed. Today, Ireland is dotted with the reminders of this age: illuminated manuscripts, simple churches, carved crosses, and about 100 round towers.

Upper Lake: The Green Road continues one mile farther up the valley to the Upper Lake. The oldest ruins—scant and hard to find—lie near this lake. If you want a scenic Wicklow walk, begin here.

NEAR DUBLIN

▲Avondale House

Located in south County Wicklow (known as the Garden County), this mansion is the birthplace and lifelong home of Charles Stewart Parnell, the Nationalist politician and dynamo often called the "uncrowned King of Ireland".

Upon entering the opulent Georgian "big house" (built in 1777), you'll first view an informative 20-minute video on Parnell's life. Then you're set free to roam with a handout outlining each room's highlights. A fine portrait of Parnell graces the grand high-ceilinged entry hall, and a painting of his American grandfather, who manned the USS *Constitution* in the War of 1812, hangs in one room. The dining room is all class, with fine plasterwork and hardwood floors. Original furniture such as Parnell's sturdy canopied bed graces the remaining rooms, and many come with cozy fireplaces and views. The lush surrounding estate of over 500 acres, laced with pleasant walking trails, was used by the Irish Forestry Service (Coillte) to try out forestry methods.

Cost and Hours: €6.50; June Tue-Sun 11:00-16:00, closed Mon; July-Aug daily 11:30-16:30; Sept-Oct Sat-Sun 12:00-16:00, closed Mon-Fri; shorter hours off-season; café, tel. 0404/46111, www.coillteoutdoors.ie.

Getting There: A visit is best done by car, as it's too far for the Dublin day-tour buses (45 miles south of Dublin). Trains depart Dublin's Connolly station (4/day, 1.5 hours) to Rathdrum; Avondale is a short taxi ride away (1.5 miles south of town).

West of Dublin:
The Irish National Stud

Ireland's famed County Kildare has long been known to offer the perfect conditions for breeding horses. Its reputation dates all the way back to the 1300s, when Norman war horses were bred here. Kildare's grasslands lie on a bedrock table of limestone, infusing the soil with just the right mix of nutrients for grazing horses. And the nearby River Tully sparkles with high levels of calcium carbonate, essential for building strong bones in the expensive thoroughbreds (some owned by Arab sheiks) raised and raced here.

In 1900, Colonel William Hall-Walker (Scottish heir to the Johnny Walker distilling fortune) bought a farm on the River Tully and began breeding a line of champion thoroughbreds. His amazing successes and bizarre methods were the talk of the sport. In 1916, the colonel donated his land and horse farm to the British government, which continued breeding horses here. The farm was eventually handed over to the Irish government, which in 1945 created the Irish National Stud Company to promote the thoroughbred industry.

Today, a tour of the grounds at the Irish National Stud gives you a fuller appreciation for the amazing horses that call this place home. Animal-lovers and horse-racing fans driving between Dublin and Galway will enjoy a couple of hours here, combining the tour with lunch (inside the decent cafeteria or at a picnic table by the parking lot) and a stroll through the gardens.

Cost and Hours: €11 includes guided tour of the Irish National Stud, plus entry to Japanese Gardens, St. Fiachra's Garden, and Horse Museum; open daily early Feb-mid-Dec 9:30-18:00, closed mid-Dec-early Feb, last entry one hour before closing, 30-minute tours run 3/day at 12:00, 14:30, and 16:00. Tel. 045/522-963, www.irish-national-stud.ie.

Getting to the Irish National Stud: From M7, **drivers** take exit #13 and follow the signs five minutes south (don't take exit #12 for the Curragh Racecourse). **Trains** departing Dublin's Heuston station stop at Kildare town (1-3/hour, 45 minutes, www.irishrail.ie). A shuttle bus runs from Kildare's train station to the National Stud (2/hour), or you can take a taxi (about €12-15). One **bus** departs Dublin's Busáras station Monday through Saturday at 9:30, and returns from the National Stud at 15:45. On Sunday, two buses run, departing Busáras at 10:00 and 12:00, with returns at 15:00 and 17:30. Confirm this schedule at the bus station in Dublin.

Touring the Grounds: The guided tour begins in the **Sun**

When Irish Horses Are Running

Every Irish town seems to have a betting shop for passionate locals who love to closely follow (and wager on) their favorite horses. A quick glance at the weekend sports sections of any Irish newspaper gives you an idea of this sport's high profile. Towns from Galway to Dingle host annual horse races that draw rabid fans from all over.

The five most prestigious Irish races take place at the **Curragh Racecourse,** just south of Kildare town (March-Oct, 1 hour west of Dublin, 10 minutes from the National Stud, www.curragh.ie). Horses have been raced here since 1741. The broad, open fields nearby are where the battle scenes in *Braveheart* were filmed (the neighboring Irish army base provided the blue-face-painted extras).

Chariot Yard (named for the winner of the 1942 Fillies Triple Crown), surrounded by stables housing pregnant mares. A 15-minute film of a foal's birth runs continuously in a stall in the corner of the yard.

The adjacent **Foaling Unit** is where births take place. The gestation period for horses is 11 months, with 90 percent of foals born at night. (In the wild, a mare and her foal born during the day would have been vulnerable to predators as the herd moved on. Instead, horses have adapted so that foals are born at night—and are able to keep up with the herd within a few hours.) Eccentric Colonel Walker noted the position of the moon and stars at the time of each foal's birth, and sold those born under inauspicious astrological signs (regardless of their parents' stellar racing records).

From here, you'll pass a working saddle-making shop and a forge where horseshoes are still hammered out on an anvil.

At the **Stallion Boxes,** you'll learn how stargazing Colonel Walker installed skylights in the stables—allowing the heavens maximum influence over the destiny of his prized animals. A brass plaque on the door of each stall proudly states the horse's name and its racing credentials. One stall bears the simple word, "Teaser." The unlucky occupant's job is to identify mares in heat...but rarely is the frustrated stallion given the opportunity to breed. Bummer.

After the tour, meander down the pleasant tree-lined **Tully Walk,** with paddocks on each side. You'll see mares and foals running free, with the occasional cow thrown in for good measure (cattle have a calming effect on rowdy horses). To ensure you come home with all your fingers, take full note of the *Horses Bite and Kick* signs. These superstar animals are bred for high spirits—and are far too feisty to pet.

Other Sights: Visitors with extra time can explore three more attractions (all included in your entry ticket). The tranquil and photogenic **Japanese Gardens** were created by the colonel to depict the trials of life (beware the Tunnel of Ignorance). A wander through the more extensive and natural **St. Fiachra's Garden** (the patron saint of gardening) demands more time. Equestrian buffs may want to linger among the memorabilia in the small **Horse Museum,** where you can get a grip on how many hands it takes to measure a horse.

NEAR DUBLIN

PRACTICALITIES

This section covers just the basics on traveling in Ireland (for much more information, see *Rick Steves' Ireland*). You can find free advice on specific topics at www.ricksteves.com/tips.

Money

Ireland uses the euro currency: 1 euro (€) = about $1.40. To convert prices in euros to dollars, add about 40 percent: €20 = about $28, €50 = about $70. (Check www.oanda.com for the latest exchange rates.)

The standard way for travelers to get euros is to withdraw money from a cash machine using a debit or credit card, ideally with a Visa or MasterCard logo. Before departing, call your bank or credit-card company: Confirm that your card will work overseas, ask about international transaction fees, and alert them that you'll be making withdrawals in Europe.

Your US credit card might not work at some stores or at automated machines (e.g., train and subway ticket machines, luggage lockers, toll booths, parking garages, and self-serve gas pumps), because they're designed to accept European credit cards with a PIN code. If your card doesn't work, you have several options: Pay with euros, try your PIN code (ask your credit-card company in advance or use a debit card), or find a nearby cashier who should be able to process the transaction.

To keep your valuables safe, wear a money belt. But if you do lose your credit or debit card, report the loss immediately to the respective global customer-assistance centers. Call these 24-hour US numbers collect: Visa (410/581-9994), MasterCard (636/722-7111), and American Express (623/492-8427).

Phoning

Smart travelers use the telephone to reserve or reconfirm rooms, reserve restaurants, get directions, research transportation connections, confirm tour times, phone home, and lots more.

To call Ireland from the US or Canada: Dial 011-353 and then the area code (minus its initial zero) and local number. (The 011 is our international access code, and 353 is Ireland's country code.)

To call Ireland from a European country: Dial 00-353 followed by the area code (minus its initial zero) and local number. (The 00 is Europe's international access code.)

To call within Ireland: If you're dialing within an area code, just dial the local number; but if you're calling outside your area code, you have to dial both the area code (which starts with a 0) and the local number.

To call from Ireland to another country: Dial 00 followed by the country code (for example, 1 for the US or Canada), then the area code and number. If you're calling European countries whose phone numbers begin with 0, you'll usually have to omit that 0 when you dial.

Tips on Phoning: To make calls in Ireland, you can buy two different types of phone cards—international or insertable—sold locally at newsstands. Cheap international phone cards, which work with a scratch-to-reveal PIN code at any phone, allow you to call home to the US for pennies a minute, and also work for domestic calls within Ireland. Insertable phone cards, which must be inserted into public pay phones, are reasonable for calls within Ireland (and work for international calls as well, but not as cheaply as the international phone cards). Calling from your hotel-room phone is usually expensive, unless you use an international phone card. A mobile phone—whether an American one that works in Ireland, or a European one you buy when you arrive—is handy, but can be pricey. For more on phoning, see www.ricksteves.com/phoning.

Emergency Telephone Numbers in Ireland: To summon the police or an ambulance, dial 999. For passport problems, call the **US Embassy** (in Dublin, tel. 01/668-7122 or 01/668-8777) or the **Canadian Embassy** (in Dublin, tel. 01/234-4000). For other concerns, get advice from your hotel.

Making Hotel and B&B Reservations

To ensure the best value, I recommend reserving rooms in advance, particularly during peak season. Email the hotelier or B&B host with the following key pieces of information: number and type of rooms; number of nights; date of arrival; date of departure; and any special requests. (For a sample form, see www.ricksteves.com/reservation.) Use the European style for writing dates: day/month/

year. For example, for a two-night stay in July, you could request: "1 double room for 2 nights, arrive 16/07/12, depart 18/07/12." Hoteliers typically ask for your credit-card number as a deposit.

Know the terminology: An "en suite" room has a bathroom (toilet and shower/tub) actually inside the room; a room with a "private bathroom" can mean that the bathroom is all yours, but it's across the hall; and a "standard" room has access to a bathroom that's shared with other rooms and down the hall.

In general, hotel prices can soften if you do any of the following: stay in a "standard" room, offer to pay cash, stay at least three nights, or travel off-season.

Eating

The traditional "Irish Fry" breakfast includes juice, tea or coffee, cereal, eggs, bacon, sausage, toast, a grilled tomato, sautéed mushrooms, and black pudding. If it's too much for you, just order the items you want.

To dine affordably at classier restaurants, look for "early-bird specials" (offered about 17:30–19:00, last order by 19:00). At a sit-down place with table service, tip about 10 percent—unless the service charge is already listed on the bill.

Smart travelers use pubs (short for "public houses") to eat, drink, and make new friends. Pub grub is Ireland's best eating value. For about $15–20, you'll get a basic hot lunch or dinner. The menu is hearty and traditional: stews, soups, fish-and-chips, meat, cabbage, potatoes, and—in coastal areas—fresh seafood. Order drinks and meals at the bar. Pay as you order, and don't tip.

When you say "a beer, please" in an Irish pub, you'll get a pint of Guinness. (If you think you don't like Guinness, try it in Ireland.) For a cold, refreshing, basic, American-style beer, ask for a lager, such as Harp. If you want a small beer, ask for a glass or a half-pint.

Craic (pronounced crack), Irish for "fun" or "a good laugh," means good conversation for the participants. It's the sport that accompanies drinking in a pub. People are there to talk. Don't be afraid to make new friends. To toast them in Irish, say, *"Slainte"* (SLAWN-chuh).

Traditional music is alive and popular in pubs throughout Ireland. "Sessions" (musical evenings) may be planned and advertised or impromptu. There's generally a fiddle, a flute or tin whistle, a guitar, a *bodhrán* (goatskin drum), and maybe an accordion or mandolin. Things usually get going at about 21:30. Last call for drinks is at about 23:30.

Transportation

By Car: A car is a worthless headache in Dublin. But if venturing into the countryside, I enjoy the freedom of a rental car for reaching far-flung rural sights. It's cheaper to arrange most car rentals from the US. Note that many credit-card companies do not offer collision coverage for rentals in Ireland. For tips on your insurance options, see www.ricksteves.com/cdw. Bring your driver's license. For route planning, try www.viamichelin.com.

Remember that the Irish drive on the left side of the road (and the driver sits on the right side of the car). You'll quickly master Ireland's many roundabouts: Traffic moves clockwise, cars inside the roundabout have the right-of-way, and entering traffic yields (look to your right as you merge). Note that "camera cops" strictly enforce speed limits by automatically snapping photos of speeders' license plates, then mailing them a bill.

By Train and Bus: The best overall source for public transportation schedules is the Tourism Ireland website: www.discover ireland.com (select "Plan Your Visit," then "Getting Around"). You can also check train schedules at www.irishrail.ie or listen to a recorded timetable at 01/805-4222. In Ireland, most travelers find it's cheapest simply to buy train tickets as they go. To see if a railpass could save you money, check www.ricksteves.com/rail.

Long-distance buses (called "coaches") are about a third slower than trains, but they're also much cheaper. Bus stations are normally at or near train stations. The Bus Éireann Expressway Bus Timetable is handy (free, available at some bus stations or online at www.buseireann.ie, bus info tel. 01/836-6111).

Helpful Hints

Time: Ireland uses the 24-hour clock. It's the same through 12:00 noon, then keep going: 13:00, 14:00, and so on. Ireland, like Great Britain, is five/eight hours ahead of the East/West Coasts of the US (and one hour earlier than most of continental Europe).

Holidays and Festivals: Ireland celebrates many holidays, which can close sights and attract crowds (book hotel rooms ahead). For information on holidays and festivals, check Ireland's website: www.discoverireland.com. For a simple list showing major—though not all events, see www.ricksteves.com/festivals

Numbers and Stumblers: What Americans call the second floor of a building is the first floor in Ireland. Irish people write dates as day/month/year, so Christmas is 25/12/12. For most measurements, Ireland uses the metric system: A kilogram is 2.2 pounds, and a liter is about a quart. For driving distances, the country is still transitioning from miles to kilometers (a kilometer is six-tenths of a mile).

Resources from Rick Steves

This Snapshot guide is excerpted from the latest edition of *Rick Steves' Ireland*, which is one of more than 30 titles in my series of guidebooks on European travel. I also produce a public television series, *Rick Steves' Europe*, and a public radio show, *Travel with Rick Steves*. My website, www.ricksteves.com, offers free travel information, a Graffiti Wall for travelers' comments, guidebook updates, my travel blog, an online travel store, and information on European railpasses and our tours of Europe. If you're bringing a mobile device on your trip, you can download free information from Rick Steves Audio Europe, featuring podcasts of my radio shows, free audio tours of major sights in Europe, and travel interviews and other audio content about Ireland (via www.ricksteves .com/audioeurope, iTunes, or the Rick Steves Audio Europe free smartphone app).

Additional Resources

Tourist Information: www.discoverireland.com
Passports and Red Tape: www.travel.state.gov
Packing List: www.ricksteves.com/packlist
Cheap Flights: www.skyscanner.net
Airplane Carry-on Restrictions: www.tsa.gov/travelers
Updates for This Book: www.ricksteves.com/update

How Was Your Trip?

If you'd like to share your tips, concerns, and discoveries after using this book, please fill out the survey at www.ricksteves.com/ feedback. Thanks in advance—it helps a lot.

INDEX

INDEX

Audio Europe

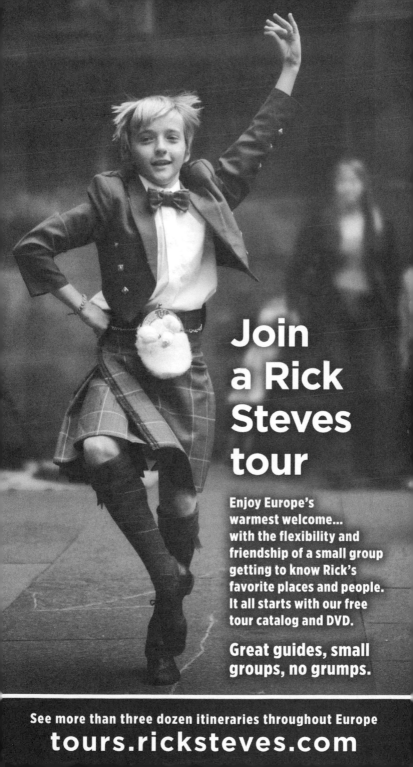

▸ Plan Your Trip

Browse thousands of articles and a wealth of money-saving tips for planning your dream trip. You'll find up-to-date information on Europe's best destinations, packing smart, getting around, finding rooms, staying healthy, avoiding scams and more.

▸ Eurail Passes

Find out, step-by-step, if a railpass makes sense for your trip—and how to avoid buying more than you need. Get free shipping on online orders

▸ Graffiti Wall & Travelers Helpline

Learn, ask, share—our online community of savvy travelers is a great resource for first-time travelers to Europe, as well as seasoned pros.

Rick Steves' Europe Through the Back Door, Inc.